The Long
and
Winding Road

Lyn Clarke

Best wishes,

Lyn Clarke

Clarke Books
Anna Maria Island, Florida

Cover, Interior and eBook design
by Blue Harvest Creative
www.blueharvestcreative.com

The Long and Winding Road

Copyright © 2012 Lyn Clarke

Published by
Clarke Books

ISBN-13: 978-0615730745
ISBN-10: 0615730744

Visit the author at:
www.clarkebooks.net

Also By Lyn Clarke

Memoirs of a Welshman
Ramblings of a Welshman
Reflections of a Welshman
Amazing States
Echoes In My Mind

Dedication

I dedicate this, my sixth book, to the wonderful people of Anna Maria Island whose generosity and kindness to me has been overwhelming. Since arriving here, some thirteen years ago, they have welcomed me with open arms and have allowed me into their homes and their hearts. Just like myself many of today's islanders are transplants, from other areas of America and even parts of Europe, and so they are passing on the generosity shown to them when they arrived here. Whether at work, home or at play they have a zest for life which is infectious and this trait makes me proud to also be considered an "islander." In all the years that I have lived here I have rarely encountered an unkind word or an unfriendly disposition. This is the fourth place that I have lived, in my nomadic life, and I have decided this will be my final resting place. When I finally go to that other island, in the sky, I have requested that my ashes be scattered over the beautiful waters of the Gulf of Mexico. This ensures that I will forever remain a part of this idyllic place. Even after death I know that I will still be connected to the place that I have grown to love and that people here will remember me with some degree of affection. My heartfelt thanks goes out to the unique people of Anna Maria Island. Who could not love a group of people whose unofficial motto is "We are a drinking island with a fishing problem."

Boy Scout Lyn and friend at fourteen years of age.

One
In the Beginning

To say that my early days, of growing up in Wales, was unusual is a vast understatement. My family was relatively poor back then and, at best, we eked out a bare existence of a life. This was brought on by my father being killed in 1943 while serving in the Royal Navy during World War II. Because of this I was brought up in a house with no men as both of my grandfathers had earlier passed away. There was my mother, my grandmother, my sister Ann who everyone called Bunny and myself. This, even as young as I was, in my mind made me the man of the house. Right after my father's demise we went to live with my Gran at Edward Street for several years. This allowed my mother to go back to work as a nurse at Panteg Hospital and, because she worked the weekend night shift, she was paid double time. In this manner she could earn almost the same amount of money, on the weekend, as she could earn in five midweek day shifts. The night shifts were quieter because most of the patients were asleep and my mother just patrolled the wards and dole out medication to those in need. This also allowed her to be home during the week and help Nana to ensure that we kids were well taken care of. When my mother finally saved up enough money, to put a deposit down on our own house up on Bushy Park, we still stayed with our grandmother on the weekends until I was around the age of fourteen. At this age my sister, who was eighteen months older than me, persuaded mother that we were now old enough to be left at home by ourselves. By now we were living down on King Street about a block from Nana's. However, we had an ulterior motive as we would sneak out on Saturday night and go to the local dance hall but we were always back in bed sleeping by the time that Mother came home around 8: 00 AM on Sunday morning. My sister had, in fact, taught me to dance at home to music on the radio and so we started the evening by dancing with each other and when we were nicely warmed up we would split up and invite others to dance. Mother never did find out about our Saturday night escapades until many years later when, in a moment of weakness, we confessed.

Food was not too plentiful in those days and although we had enough to keep us going, we kids were always hungry. When I was around six years of age my mother used to comment that I was too thin to be able to cast my own shadow. Sometimes, for a joke, she would as me to show her my muscles at which I would immediately strike one of those body builder's poses and flex my physique. My muscles resembled knots in a strand of cotton and my mother would just about bust a gut from laughing hysterically with tears rolling down her cheeks. I think she did not do this to be cruel but because she had so few things that she could laugh about, as amusement was limited, in those dark and dismal times. With all this female pampering I learned very early how to get just about anything I wanted. If my mother wouldn't give it to me I went to my Gran or on times to my sister. My mother often refered to me, on these occasions, as little Lord Fauntleroy which was basically her way of telling me that I was spoiled rotten. However, being spoiled in our family came nowhere near to what it meant for children of prosperous families. All this feminine pampering put me in good stead later in life when, as a teenager, I started to mix with the fairer sex. I was completely at home in their company and was never tongue tied or shy in their presence. It was as if something had been instilled in me, perhaps respect for the opposite sex, which rendered me completely at ease when with them. Thus, girls were drawn to me from my age of twelve onwards and I was rarely without a date from that age onward. My grandmother taught me how to darn my own socks, my mother taught me the basic rudiments of cooking and, as I have already said, my sister taught me how to dance. I had developed into a complete ladies man, so far as the opposite sex was concerned.

The other reason why I was so thin was because, up until the age of ten years old, I was quite sickly. Obviously the dreary cold temperatures and the consistent rain did not help in this respect and I always seemed to have a cold or a sore throat. At aged nine my mother somehow wangled it so that I was admitted to Panteg Hospital and had my tonsils removed. This seemed to cure me of quite a few of the maladies that I had previously been plagued with. I was also prone to getting side aches, or stitches as we called them, particularly after I had been running. So at the age of ten I was back in hospital, this time at Pontypool, having my appendix removed. After recovering from these two operations I began, for the first time, to enjoy life more and I gradually regained strength and finally started to put on some well needed weight. I graduated from a skinny little runt to a wirey but fit young man. When at sixteen I played my first game of rugby, in a men's league, I was a mere one hundred and twenty pounds wringing wet. Later on in life when I was nineteen and playing rugby up in Cheshire, England I tipped the scales at a, for me, massive weight of one hundred and sixty pounds. To this very day I still hover around that very same weight and I think that being at this low weight, for a person of five foot nine inches tall, has provided me with a good standard of health. Since those traumatic early times I have rarely been ill in the whole of my adult life and it appears that I have laid all those infant day bugaboos to rest. Another extremely important factor, for my continued good health, is that I never fell foul or became a victim of smoking cigarettes. This habit, as we have now learned, will hamper a person's health with numerous maladies and shorten their life expectancy, by a considerably amount. By not smoking my skin also remained unblemished thus causing my appearance to be younger than my actual age.

Back then, in my childhood days, on almost every Sunday afternoon my Grandma would make Welsh cakes. She called them baked stones, as they were also known, which she heated on her griddle on top of the gas stove. Each day I would take a couple of them to school to eat for my lunch along with a bottle of milk which the school provided. During those times milk was about the only regular thing that we had for obtaining a source of Vitamin C which assure that we had sturdy bones and strong teeth. My Gran also made all her own jams and my particular favorite was her gooseberry concoction. It was somewhat tart to the taste but it did ensure that my toilet regimen was always regular and in good working order. On occasions I would find a free range chicken, duck or goose egg and would bring it home for my supper. Back then we did not buy peas or beans from a supermarket in cans. We bought them from the farmers market in their pods and it was the job of my sister and I to shell them. During this process I would frequently chew on the pods to extract the juices from them as I enjoyed their distinct dentine like flavor. However I would spit out the chewed up pods as they were difficult to swallow and hard to digest. On the few occasions that we had meat for dinner, usually beef, my mother would drain off the hot liquid fat into a jar and let it set for a few days. When food was short she would spread this on slices of bread for us to eat. This we called a dripping sandwich which was salty and had no nutritional value as far as I know. All this food did was to fill a hole in our empty stomachs and, in so doing, prevent them from rumbling. Every once in a while my mother would splash out and buy some fruit like oranges, bananas or strawberries but for apples we kids would raid the local orchards. Unfortunately these were the shiny green cooking apples which, when eaten raw, gave us the tummy gripes. The only time that we realy enjoyed them was when they were cored and baked in the oven with a sprinkling of sugar. This was the nearest thing that we ever saw that resembled a dessert and these events were rare and eagerly anticipated.

In spite of the rigors of this era we still somehow were able to survive and perhaps we learned to appreciate the few pleasures that came our way. I can still remember one particular Christmas when my sister and I received, in our stockings, an orange, a pear, a bar of chocolate, a drawing book and some crayons as this was all that our mother could afford. These times were not quite as bad as the Great Depression that occurred in America in the 1930's but our lot was not a very fruitful one. Never-the-less, we kids were blissfully happy and unaware of most of the troubles and strife that blighted our lives. We were the epitome of the saying that there are none so blind as those who will not see. After about four years of living up on Bushy Park our family moved down from the mountain into a small corner shop in King Street. This put us just a hundred yards from grandmother's house and my sister and I went over to her house whenever we felt like doing so. That woman was a great influence in our otherwise dull lives. She was so loving and, in all the years of me knowing her, I did not hear her say an unkind word about anyone. She was generous to a fault and often gave away to others, on a daily basis, what little she owned. She opened her house to friends and strangers alike and never asked for anything in return. If there is a heaven where angels exist, I am certain that she is up there amongst them because, in my experience, there never was a more loving and kind person in the world.

The one thing that I did not like, about the area where I grew up, was the fist fighting culture that abounded back then.

Throwing the occasional punch during a heated exchange on the rugby field was one thing but standing toe to toe and slugging it out was a horse of another color. From the age of around twelve years onwards, some boys would call you out if you so much as gave them a sideward glance or for some other ridiculous reason. Some days walking around Pontypool was like stepping on hot coals and when two egos collided, over some trivial matter, just like back at The O.K. Corral the fight was on right there and then. You could not openly speak your mind, concerning anyone, for fear that it would upset someone who would become offended and then come looking for you. They would literally hunt you down to confront you and the only choices available were fight, apologize or run for your life and hope that you were faster than your pursuer. The main reason for me finding myself in these unenviable of all situatios was from flirting with the fairer sex. Because of my many involvements with girls, from all over the area, I often found myself face to face with a perfect stranger not knowing why. If a certain boy was trying to date the girl of his choice and she told him that she preferred me, this put me in the direct line of fire. I frequently stood up for myself and, on occasions, the aggressor would stand down. However, if we fought and I won sometimes that challenger's brother or best pal would then come looking for me to settle the score. You were damned if you did and damned if you didn't.

There was also gang fights where one group of boys, from a specific street or area, would fight another similar gang over an insult or some minor indiscretion or other. If you won, as a gang or on your own, just like in the Old West the toughies from miles around would then come looking to put a notch on their belts. Just before I left Pontypool I had some of the meanest guys, in our valley, trying to catch up with me to settle some scores. This, in no small way, was part of the reason why I moved away and left all such problems behind. This culture was foreign, to my new surrounds, and it was so nice not having to constantly watch over my shoulder. My dating exploits did not change but, in Cheshire, I had two plus conditions in my favor. I was an unknown quantity to the male population and the people there were much more civilized when it came to settling disputes. As the old saying goes"It is better the devil that you know, than the devil you don't know."

Two
An Era of Note

As a teenager growing, up in my hometown of Pontypool, life was exciting, The town was vibrant and bustling with business. Hardly anyone had their own transport back then and so the shoppers would pour in by bus from the surrounding areas. They would come down the hills, from The Tranch and Wainfelin and from Penygarn and Trevethin. They would come down the valley from as far up as Abersycan and up the valley from as far down as Sebasapol. They would virtually pour off the buses and flood the sidewalks and small shops. The butcher, the baker and even the candlestick maker, all extracted their pound of flesh. People would bring their own shopping baskets or those deep cloth shopping bags and by the time they boarded their bus, for home, these would be full to the brim. Because refrigeration was not prevalent back then people shopped almost every day. This very fact made them more sociable and kept them skinny and fit. To see a fat person back then was a rarity and obese people had not yet been invented. The people who grew up during those times are still relatively thin, to this very day, unfortunately they are gradually dying off and becoming as extinct as the dinosaurs.

In those times our town and surrounding area had about forty to fifty churches of just about every possible denomination. There must have been around almost one hundred ale houses selling a plethora of different brands of beer. We had three movie houses, or cinemas as they were called, and four if you include the one in Griffithstown We had our very own dance hall and two rugby teams the one Pontypool R.F.C played down in the Town Park and the other Pontypool United, or Harlequins as they were known prior to World War II, played at the Recreation Ground up on School Lane, Wainfelin. Both teams wore the traditional black, white and red hooped shirts which, when seen, instilled fear into the hearts of opposing teams. The town team also had their very own Supporters Club House down near the north park gate entrance. This was considered a Mecca to rugby fans from around the world. So good was our town team that it played against international sides, the last being Australia in 1986, and it was quite common to have 20,000 spectators attending these prestigious games. I know this for a fact because as a kid and I would attend these epic struggles. Almost all of our town's rugby players were born and bred within about five miles of the club house and so we all grew up together. Occasionally a player from another town would join our club to enhance his chances of being selected for the Welsh National Team which was, and still is, a great honor. However the players of these rare exceptions had to be of exceptional quality to be selected over a home grown player.

In these current times my home town is a ghost town when compared to those hallcean days. Nearly all of the churches are gone and so conversely are most of the ale houses. Because of the stigma of a possible drink/driving ban people now only go to the surviving pubs and working men's clubs in the surrounding hills. Very few people venture down town anymore as it is much more practical to walk to a neighborhood pub and then confidently stroll home after a social drink with ones friends. The non-smoking ban has also had its affect on these pub scene plus the fact the you can go to the local liquor store and buy an eight pack, of sixteen ounce beers, for six pounds. This is seventy five pence each, for a drink that would cost around four times more expensive at an ale house. In other words two pub drinks are the same price as eight from the store and the math is clearly simple. The only other survivors of this modern phenomenon are the posh country pubs that have extensive dinner menus and where a family can go to celebrate a special event. Otherwise it is a gloom and doom scenario particularly because there are no longer any cinemas, dance halls or even a rugby supporters club left in existence. Even the towns centuries old Market is hanging on by a thread because the town councilors decided, in there infinite wisdom, to allow outside traders to come into the town on certain days of the week and sell their wares in the street. At the end of the day they take all the money, from that days trading, and leave without spending one penny back into the town. To add to all this decay two large multi-stores have moved into town and most of the family owned shops have slowly disappeared. A new shopping mall, mostly covered from the incessant rain, was built in Cwmbran just four miles south and so it is now more convenient to drive and shop there. Especially since a by-pass road has been built and it is no longer necessary to drive through Pontypool, which can now be conveniently avoided all together. The people of my generation still remember the good old days in the history of our town. I guess for the current people, under fifty years old, who still live there, it is a case of what you don't know can't hurt you. For them these seemingly harmless but, in the long term, drastic changes are part of a progression of events that just happened.

These events have unwittingly ripped the heart out of a once vibrant town. For someone like me, who moved away many years ago and can only visits once a year, these changes appear disastrous. For the people who have stayed at home the gradual changes have hardly been notice to any great extent. When they see all the boarded up empty stores and the preponderance of resale shops, in their midst, it must beg the question as to the well being of the community. One old timer recently said to me, on my most recent visit, that even the resale shops are now closing down due to lack of business. If this is not an indication, concerning the down fall of a once proud town, I don't know what is.

I do hope no-one back home takes offense by my comments because this is my honest assessment of the facts that have undeniably occurred over the last thirty to forty years. Change is not always made for the good and if the decisions are controlled by inexperienced people this type of urban decay becomes the inevitable result. I realize the our town has lost its two main industries, that of coal mining and steel manufacturing but this void was never filled by other forms of industry. For example the industrious city of Pittsburgh, here in America, has gone through the exact same set of circumstances but today, some thirty years later, it is back to being a thriving and energetic environment. Pittsburgh is probably ten times bigger than Pontypool and yet, like the phoenix that arose from the ashes, it has They have been successful and came back from the brink of despair and out of desperate times. Perhaps I can be accused of living in the past but it grieves me greatly to see my once proud home town in the abyss of conplacencey. I hope my avid viewpoints will be taken in the manner in which they were intended. I now live in Florida, some three thousand plus miles away, and so it would be naïve of me to think that I can assist in the solving of these problem. It is easy to criticize from afar, it is entirely another thing completely to be able to reverse the current mode of local government operations.

At the next town mayoral election it is imperative to elect a person who can not only talk the talk and the elected person must also be able to make sweeping changes. This must be done in a workman like manner so that these important issues are taken care of. He, or she, must be a person of decisive action, impervious to criticism and be a visionary who can devise a five year forward plan and take the town to where it needs to be. Most importantly, this plan must be achieved. I hope that this can be attained because something simply must be done to bring back the pride that we once had in our town's reputation. Perhaps this complicated job should be handled by a complete outsider. Someone like a business consultant who can put aside the past transgressions and take an objective look at the situation without being swayed by previous bad judgments. Surely there must be some bright eyed, eager ex Pontypool born degreed person out there somewhere who could fit the bill. Let us hope so because the revitalization of our town is of prime importance to us all. God bless Pontypool and all who have her best interests at heart. While we are on the subject of pandemonium, do you really think that this can be caused by pandas.

I now live in America and I have just found out a very interesting connection between my home town and the USA which occurred in the terrible American Civil War, circa 1861 to 1865, when brothers fought brothers. There was a Union general namesWilliam Powell and the history books have him originating from the town of Pontypwl. He was wounded and captured at the battle of Wytheville, Virginia. He was revered so much by the northern Union Army that he was swapped out of prison in return for the son of none other than Robert E. Lee the Supreme Commander of the Southern Confederate Army. History shows that there were many Welsh born soldiers who served in the following regiments during that conflict. The 9th Pennsylvania, the 117th and the 146th New Yorker, the 9th Minnesota, the 22nd Wisconsin and the 56th Ohio. What the history books do not tell is how many of those brave men lost there lives in that horrific conflict.. In one location alone around fifty thousand Americans lost their lives at the three day battle of Gettysburg, Pennsylvania.

Another Pontypool born man of note was named Morgan Edwards. He emigrated to America and became the founder of the prestigious Brown University at the city of Providence, in the State of Rhode Island. Now, there is some earth shattering revelation that can stun your neighbors at the next local social gathering. I realize that the American Civil War is not exactly top of most people's conversation list but what a breath of fresh air this will inject into the proceedings. I can almost hear the gasps of surprise emanating from the meeting place in between sips of tea. I am sure the response from the attendees will be the word that all Welsh people always say when a new and stunning piece of information is revealed...Never!

Three
Rugby Crazy

Pontypool, in the past, had the reputation of being one of the top town rugby clubs on the planet and was well revered around the globe by many power house rugby nations. Over those years almost two hundred Pontypool men have been selected to play for their country and for a Welshman there is no greater honor. To represent Wales, in an international match, is the dream of just about every young Welsh boy from the time that he straps on his first pair of rugby boots. Those Pontypool rugby players, who were awarded this distinction, have done our country proud and upheld a noble tradition.

My father was the captain of the Harlequins, the other Pontypool club, directly before it was temporarily disbanded during World War II. Unfortunately he never returned from that great fiasco and so his rugby playing days was curtailed. If he had survived that war he would have taken up where he left off back with that same team. The only difference was that the club's name was forever changed from Harlequins to United to honor the fact that the players represented just about every division of the armed forces. When my mother passed away some ten years ago I found, in her meager possessions, a faded and tattered piece of paper listing the Pontypool Harlequins team players for selection to play against Pontnewydd back in 1939. The players were R. Stokes, E. J. Britten, D. Constance, J. Tucker, D. Bryant, H. Gibson, L. Daniels, L. Clarke, R. Constance, A. Harris, N. Parry, D. Francis, E. W. Paynter, F. Davies, N. Sullivan, L. Wilson, R. Munn, C. Smith and J. Simmons. Perhaps, for some people, a few of these names might stir up some lost memories of yesteryear. I remember that when I was around eight or nine years of age the United team went two seasons without defeat and this included playing such teams as Newport United and Gloucester United. Another undefeated Welsh rugby team of that era was Glyneath and I was at the Recreation Ground the day United beat them in a very close match. For many years they were a rugby power house and this continued for several decades.

How different my life would have been if my father was not killed. I probably would not have left my home town, at the age of nineteen, as I did. Instead of joining Girling's as an apprentice and signing an agreement with them that I would only play rugby for them in the Newport league, I would have played youth rugby for Pontypool. Who knows with my father's contacts, in the local rugby circles, I might even have ended up playing for the Ponypool town team. Several of my pals from the Girling rugby team did just that and they often told me that, if I had stayed at home, I had the skills to have done the same. Although I played some excellent rugby with several teams, up in Cheshire and Lancashire, I always had that nagging feeling of what could have been if I had stayed in Pontypool. My old coach Jack Harris has, up until just recently, told a good friend of mine that in his opinion I might have even represented my country, as an international player, if I had stayed in Wales.

When I was seventeen years of age I was walking through the town with my kit bag over my shoulder. I had to catch a bus down to Newport to play against the Saracens of that town. I bumped into one of my old Abersychan school mates and he asked where I was going. I told him that I had to play a rugby match in Newport and on my merry way I went. For several weeks after that encounter quite a few people, who would normally speak to me, passed by me without saying a word. Finally I cornered one of them and I asked why he had snubbed me. He said that there was a rumor going around the town that I was a traitor and was playing rugby for a Newport team. In Pontypool this was just about the biggest sin that any rugby player could commit. Apparently when I told the original guy that I was playing rugby"in"Newport he told everybody that I was playing"for"Newport. In Pontypool we called the Newport team"those black and amber bastards"and so for one of our home grown players to represent them was deemed a fate worse than death. This accurately summed up the resentment that the Pontypool people felt for our, so called, illustrious neighbors from down the valley. The games between these two towns were like blood baths with no love lost and no quarter given.

I have previously said that there has been many famous rugby players who have come out of Pontypool probably none better known, around the world, than the mighty Ray Prosser. In one victorious Welsh international match Pontypool supplied six of the fifteen players and five of them were playing in the pack of marauding forwards. I could spend hours naming all the individual players and their exploits but instead I want to zero in on a player who has, in no small way, changed the game of rugby for ever. This particular player was selected for our county of Monmouthshire, as it was called before being changed back to the Celtic name of Gwent. However this player was never selected for Wales much to his chagrin. The person that I am referring to is, none other than, Ray Cheyne who played full back for Pontypool during the late 1950's and early 1960's. Ray Cheyne was the first rugby player to revolutionize the style of place kicking by approaching the ball in a soccer fashion. By this I mean that up until then all the place kickers approached the ball straight on and literally toed the ball. Ray's style was different because he approached the ball by running in an arc and hit the ball with his instep as in a soccer style By approaching the ball in a"around the corner"fashion, he could kick with greater distance and I even seen him, in one game, kick a field goal from inside his own half and right out on the touch line. This kick was from around sixty to seventy yards away from the posts and he made it with about ten yards to spare. The Pontypool crowd of supporters would chant out his name when any penalties were given around the halfway line to encourage Ray to take a kick at goal. They would go crazy if he successfully converted them. Today and for many years since Ray Cheyne began this style of kicking, all of the best kickers in the game, from around the world, have copied Ray's method and most of them have never ever heard of him.I wanted to give credit to this Pontypool player because this little known fact deserves all the accolades that it can garner. This fact should be noted by rugby players and fans across the ages as Ray Cheyne was the fore runner of all modern rugby place kickers and he should be given the credit that he so rightly deserves.

After leaving for England, at the age of nineteen, I became the designated place kicker for every rugby team that I played for up until I moved to America in 1976 which ended my playing days. In any given season I consistently tallied around one hundred points. What with the points accumulated from touch downs, drop kicks and place kicks, both penalties and conversions, this was possible. Today it is not uncommon for the best rugby players to top between two and three hundred points in a season. However, it should be noted that a lot has change in recent years. A touch down which was three points is now five points and this had to be changed because a field goal, in points, should never have equaled a touch down. Kickers today are allowed to use a tee to support the ball whereas I had to kick the ball off the ground. In my day if you were tackled just short of the line a scrum was given where the ball touched the ground. Today even though the ball touches the ground short of the line a player is allowed to slide across the goal line and a touchdown is given. Back then the linesmen could only indicate where the ball went out of play. Today they are used as two additional referees which could have prevented many off the ball fouls which were perpetrated against me when the referee was unsighted. Oh, incidentally, in my day the game of rugby was of amateur status and so all of the players worked a full time job of at least five days a week. Today the game is a professional sport and rugby is a player's full time job for which they are handsomely paid. For all of those hospital passes, broken bones, torn muscles, cuts, stitches, kicks and black eyes, I received not a single penny. Back then we played for the love of the game and our loyalties went to our home town and not to the highest bidder.

A few years ago I was at the Pontypool Supporters Club, back before it closed, when after the game a taxi driver came in and announced that he was there to pick up the players who needed to go back to Cardiff. Five players, from that days Pontypool team, got up and left taking with them all their players wages to spend in their town and not ours. Yet another case of Pontypool money going into the pockets of people who will take it else where to spend. Incidentally that very same building now stands empty and delapitated and serves as a further reminder of our town's rampant mismanagement. I have heared, just in the last month, that the future of Pontypool RFC is now in the balance and unless something desparate happens, this too could go the way of all flesh. Pontypool without a top fight rugby team is something that I cannot imagine. I hope and pray that this can be avoided because, where many people are concerned, this will be the final nail in the coffin for Ponypool. Although I am sure the people will struggle on without their team, just as Abertillery has, this is just one more avenue of enjoyment that will be closed from them. You might just as well roll up the side walk, lock up the town and throw away the key. I have a Pontypool Supporter's medallion, dated 1923-24 which I wear on a chain around my neck. No matter what the outcome of our town's demise is I will wear this keepsake there forever during my lifetime. Just to touch this good luck charm brings wonderful memories, flooding back, from those halcyon days of yester years.

Four

Heavenly Body

There comes a time in a young man's life when all is revealed. It is similar to a moment when the deepest of the World's secrets are laid bare.. At seventeen there was no greater mystery to me than a woman's body. My epiphany happened on an occasion when I took a summer vacation, for three weeks, down on the Italian Riviera with four of my close male friends. For working class boys this was the trip of a lifetime and not too many of our peers, at that time, would even contemplate such an audacious adventure. However, at that time our bunch of rapscallions always was a little different than most other young men in our home land of Wales. I, in fact, had done this trip the previous year and had so much fun that I persuaded my buddies to come along. The Mediterranean Sea, the sun, the hot sand, the tanned young women with there bikinis was so intoxicating. I talked about this so much that my pals could no longer resist the temptation of seeing these sights, for themselves, and revel in these experiences.

We flew into the French city of Nice and then traveled, by bus, along the French Riviera, with its casino towns of Canne and Menton, then on through Monte Carlo in Monaco. We crossed the Italian border via San Remo and on to our destination of

Arma di Tagia, a little town on the coast, nestled at the foothills of the Maritime Alps. About thirty minutes after checking into our hotel we were out of the door and down onto the beach and taking in all the colorful sights and, more noticeably, the smiling senoritas. It was crowded with Italian families who had headed south from the industrial cities to the north of their country. There were, of course, a large number of teenage girls and boys and it was not too long before our gang was deeply involved in beach games with them. We would all amuse ourselves by playing beach and water games which would go on for hours and the excitement was palpable. One day, as usual, there was about thirty of us teenagers, boys and girls, all frolicking about in the sea. We had divided up into two mixed teams and the one team had to keep a beach ball away from their opponents. The mixture of the English and Italian languages added to the confusion and the game became quite competitive. There was a good deal of jumping, diving, splashing and wrestling going on in an attempt to keep the ball away from the opposing teams.

On the opposing team from me was one particularly attractive, well developed, shapely Italian girl from Milan. Her name was Bianca and she looked like a model who had just stepped out of a fashion magazine. She was just an absolute joy to behold for an impressionable young man such as me. At one particular incident, during the game, she and one of the opposing team members disappeared under the water as they wrestled for possession of the ball. When they emerged Biance stood there minus her bikini top which had broken loose during the scuffle. Her extraordinary bosoms were bare to the world and I was absolutely amazed and, as you can imagine, this was a pivotal moment at this time of my young life. At that time I considered myself to be quite the ladies man and back in my home town I was considered to be quite"the lad about town"having a string of young ladies at my disposal and in the 'boy meets girl"department I was ahead of most others. I was, in fact, pretty familiar with the female breasts and was very enamored with them. However, up until this point my experiences with them had been mainly limited to some occasional quick gropes which mainly occurred while kissing and with my eyes closed. The Bianca event was entirely different because she was standing just a few feet away, in broad daylight, and had her back arched upwards while pushed her hair away from her face. She stood there with her beautiful full breasts glistening in the sun as beads of water rolled down from them. Her breasts were a wonder to behold as they were firm and pear shaped with the most audacious nipples that any boy, of my age, could imagine. I gazed at them for what seemed an eternity, which I am sure in real time, was all of ten seconds.

At this juncture one of the Italian boys alerted her to the fact that she was revealing all from the waist up. She calmly lowered her upper body below the water, replaced her malfunctioned bikini top and emerged again as calmly as if nothing had happened. To her it was nothing more than a slightly embarrassing occurrence which should not be given any particular attention. She coyly smiled and was so cool about the whole incident that I fell in lust with her right there and then. Seeing her bountiful breasts at close range in full frontal nudity changed my view of all women forever. This riveting moment taught me that a woman's body can be a thing of beauty and should be revered. Perhaps it was because she was a perfect specimen of womanly beauty or because she was so sun tanned and the picture of health. but whatever this was it left a lasting impression in my mind. One which is indelibly imprinted there upon and not forgotten some fifty years later. From that day forth I became a bosom junkie and I felt the urge to reacquaint myself with them, in a most inquisitive manner, at regular intervals. I still, to this day, get that adrenalin rush when I clap eyes on any of those wonderful unveiled appendages.

I often think of Blanca, that young feminine free spirit and this incident is now just a distant memory yet it continues to haunt me and burn brightly in my mind. I can still picture her body rising out of the ocean like a goddess. I can still picture the globules of water running down her body and dripping from her breasts. She was a magnificent young specimen of womanhood with a body of an Amazon. Without knowing it she changed my perception of women and the whole transformation only took ten seconds. From that point forward I have enjoyed watching any women's morning ritual of loading their breasts into their brassieres. I greatly appreciate and admired the fact that they carry them for the good of man kind.How clever of God to bestow the female body with not one but two of these succulent appendages. There is no doubt that from that very moment I became, if you'll excuse the pun, a sucker for a good pair of breasts. Bianca performed a wonderful miracle, one that keeps on giving and I thank her from the bottom of my heart."Bianca, Bianca, where fore art thou Blanca?"

On another occasion myself and two different friends took a weekend trip by car to London. We had very little money but wanted to experience life in the big city, or"The Smoke"as the Londoners used to call it. We spent most of our visit walking around and checking out all of the famous places that we had only previously seen in the movies or on television. The ritziest part of the enormous city is the West End and this is where all of the cinemas, night clubs and theaters are congregated. We didn't have money enough to allow us inside any of these expensive places but just standing outside of them, with all their glistening neon lights, was joy a plenty for us raw small town boys.

We were all standing outside one such establishment and I was so agog with the shear thrill of it all that I hadn't realized that my two other pals had moved on to the next sight just about twenty yards away. While I was standing there, on my own, out of nowhere came a young man in his early twenties. Thinking that I was totally alone he asked me if I liked films. When I enthusiastically told him that I did he asked me if I would like to go with him, to his apartment, where we could have a few drinks and watch a movie. I could still see my pals, who were just a short distance away and when I shouted for them, to come over to meet my new benefactor, he took off like a a bat out of hell. It then dawned on my simple rural mind that he was gay and was actually propositioning me as a prelude to a sexual encounter. Being from a small town, where everyone knew everyone else, and being barely sixteen I had never experienced such a thing before in my life. This incident taught me the lesson that everything is not what it might appear to be on the surface. From that day forth I became wise to the ways of malfunctioning people. I guess that I am just a hetrosexual kind of guy or, as my many travels since those naïve days have molded me to be, a metro sexual kind of guy. Each to his own but I do not understand why any other man would prefer the male body to that of a female. I also cannot understand why a woman would prefer a woman when God has made the female and male forms that fit so perfectly together. This practice puts the survival of the human race in jeopardy. I guess this could be summed up as the difference between"mystify"and my stiffy"...i.e. just one "f."

Lyn and Sharon at Tiger Stadium. Detroit, Michigan

Lyn and cronies at Karaoke

Lyn and Sharon at Sloppy Joe's in Key West, Florida.

The bride goes wild.

Five
The Troubled Trip

I once told a friend of mine that my father died in World War II while serving in the Shetland Islands. which is north of Scotland but south east of Iceland. He told me that he once, a long time ago, visited that frozen waste land up there in the Northern Atlantic. I asked him what ill fated turn of events led him to go to such a cold and distant place, to which he told me this story. My friend Frank's grand mother and some of his distant relatives actually lived up there in the great white north. He had never previously met any of them but when the grandmother passed away his mother sent him and his younger brother up there to represent the Welsh half of the family. His mother had been bequeathed some inheritance and so she sent the boys up to that distant place to collect it and show their respects to the old lady. Frank agreed but had some reservations because for one he and his brother had never seen eye to eye and, secondly, the Shetlands were a remote place to get to. Because of the bad blood, between him and his brother, the round trip was not going to be an easy affair. The trip was going to put them in close quarters, for around a week, which was something that they normally would have avoided, at all costs, during that tenuous period of their lives.

Getting to the Shetlands back then was no easy task. They would have to go by train from Cardiff in Wales to Aberdeen in Scotland with two train changes at Birmingham and Edinburgh in between. This was an all day journey and although they set out early in the morning they arrived in Aberdeen, tired and weary, around eight o'clock in the evening. They then had to find somewhere to stay for the night before taking the sea ferry early the next morning from Aberdeen to Lerwick, the main town in the Shetland Isles. They finally found a bed and breakfast house where they could stay for the night but because it was only a B & B they then had to go out to find somewhere to buy an evening meal. For some reason they felt somewhat uneasy with their choice of accomodation but it was too late to find anywhere else. They had this eerie feeling that they were being watched and so, before they went out for dinner, they hid their money under, not in, one of the dresser drawers in their bedroom. When they returned from dinner they checked the drawer and, sure enough, the contents had been disturbed but on checking futher their money was still there and had not been found.

They did not sleep well that night and after an early breakfast they hurriedly left to catch the ferry. As they were saying farewell to the landlady, at the front doorsteps of that establishment, her teenaged son who was retarded, stood inside at the front bay window. As Frank glanced back, on leaving, he saw the retarded boy waving goodbye while wearing Frank's brand new gloves which he had especially purchased for this northern trip. The gloves had never even been worn and the boy had one on each hand while they were still joined together by that piece of string which the maker attached so that they do not become separated prior to being sold. There he was, in all his glory, waving goodbye with the stolen evidence still on his hands and the string still joining them together. Frank had fleetingly thoughts about going back for the gloves but he was pressed for time and didn't want an ugly scene when they would have had to pry the gloves from the retarded boys hands. If this particular infringement went before a judge the result would be, if you will excuse the pun, an obvious case with strings attached. Frank thought that discretion would be the better part of valor and let the whole matter drop.

The extremely rough ferry crossing of the North Atlantic Ocean from the mainland of Scotland north to the Shaggy Isles, took around four hours of fighting off sea sickness. They both arrived the worse for wear at Lerwick which is equally as close to Oslo, Norway as it is to Scotland. There they were met by their distant relatives who spoke some strange language which sounded like a cross between Scottish and Norwegian. The communication between the Welsh visitors and these half Viking people was limited at best. At supper that night they were asked if they would like some"sprots,"a food which they conceived as being potatoes. However, when the food arrived, at the table, they were in fact some form of small fish in oil with the heads and tails still in tact. Frank and his brother politely declined this offering while their northern kin swallowed them down whole while wiping the dripping oil from their chins. During their stay there were many instances of misunderstanding and it would be a stretch of the imagination for anyone to think that they had all originated from the same family. After several days had passed and the funeral had been exorcised and the inheritance had been secured, Frank and his brother began to relax somewhat but resorted to eating, as often as possible,away from the family domain.

Towards the end of their four day stay they became bold enough to even go into some of the local bars for a few pints of beer. One night they entered one such seedy establishment to find that there was a dance party going on. As the evening progressed Frank and his brother noticed a gaunt looking person who appeared malnourished and was wearing one of those old styled donkey jackets which was tattered and torn. This person was paying particular attention to them and it was difficult for them to ascertain whether the person was male or female. As the wild and scratchy music increased in volume and the alcohol reached a plateau of insecurity, things started to come unglued. The apparition stood up and glided over to where they were sitting and grabbed the hand of Frank's younger brother and dragged him onto the dance floor. The brother was in a state of shock and did not know how to hold his wiley partner or even whether he should lead or be led. While all this was going on Frank was laughing so hard that he almost bust his gut. When Franks brother returned to their table, all pale and shivery, they beat a rapid retreat and exited the bar post haste. His brother made Frank swear, on pain of death, that he would never tell a sole about this unsavory incident. However, because of their past animosities, Frank made his siblin squirm every time the Shetlands trip was brought up in conversation. He so enjoyed watching his brother sweat bullets at the thought that he would spill the beans. Remember the age old adage that evil comes to he that evil does.

Because of the rigors of traveling the North Sea by ferry the brothers decided to spend the extra money and fly back from Lerwick to Aberdeen. Soon after take off the flight attendant asked if they would like a cocktail. Frank's brother had no money left and refused the offer but Frank, still having some money, accepted the libation. As a matter of fact he had several during the journey but he never offered to buy his wayward brother any. It wasn't until the train journey, south from Aberdeen, that Frank revealed to his brother that the drinks on the flight were complimentary and he could have requested as many as his little heart desired, This did nothing to cement their relationship and. Frank's brother did not speak to him for the duration of their ten hour train journey back to Wales. The brother was not able to tell a living sole about Frank's unkindly ruse because he still had the"creature from the bar"story hanging over his head. It was a true Mexican stand-off where each party was afraid to flinch incase it would cause the other to react in an unkindly manner. Frank, as a young man, always had flair for the dramatic and had the ability to concuct the most bizarre situation out of the most mundane of circumstances.

This sequence of events happened some forty years ago during which time, I am sure, that the Shetland islanders have advanced in step with their surrounding neighbors. In relating this story I want to clearly state that no offence is intented to this hardy breed of people who I hope to meet there myself one day soon. There is a plaque there, that my father's name is on, which is on display in Lerwick's harbor. It commemorates the fact that he and his brother seamen, gave their lives so that we all can live in a better world. I am thankful to think that this hardy and fiercely independent people have seen fit to immortalize my father's name in this manner.At this very moment, sitting here in Florida, I can visualize a Scottish piper standing on a lonely headland playing"Will You Na'er Come Back Again"and this vision, alone, gives me goose bumps.

Six
Galvanizing Moments

When growing up, in our lives, we all have had moments that, when looked back on, have shaped our lives and taught us things that we have never forgotten. Some of these experiences have guided us throughout our times and taught us valuable life lessons which have stayed with us throughout our lives. The first of mine happened when I was around the age of eight years old. I had been playing soccer with my street pals and had come into the back yard to use the outside toilet. Incidentally I didn't live in a house with an inside toilet until I left home at the age of nineteen --but I digress. I was in a great hurry to get back out to the street because my team, the black shoes, were beating the other team, the brown shoes, by two goals to one. In my rush to pee, get it over with, and get back into action I made the most fatal of all mistakes when I caught the skin of my wiener in the steel zipper of my trousers. Oh calamity of calamities, the pain was excruciating and even worse I was afraid to try to release the zipper incase I caused irreparable damage. Now this was one heck of a predicament for an eight year old boy to find himself in. Thoughts, such as, would I lose my future manhood, have I ruined a perfectly good pair of trousers and how could I possibly ask my mother for help, all flashed through my troubled mind.

After weighing up all my options, which basically came down to weather I should release the zipper slowly or fast, I took the bull by the horns and pulled it down fast. The pain was horrendous and I let out a blood curdling scream enough to scare the neighborhood cats to death. I stayed in the toilet for a further ten miutes while I handled the pain. Then I limped into the house and went to bed telling my mother that I was not feeling very well. Which actually was no lie because the incident had made me feel sick to my stomache. The lessons I learned that day was always wear underpants and always ensure that you never take your eye off the ball. Whenever I see a rugby, soccer, baseball or even basket ball player make a great play I always think to myself"I bet he never got his wiener skin caught in his zipper"More often than not, I bet that I am right. This story could be considered both historical and hysterical all at the same time, somewhat like killing two birds with one stone.

I attended Abersychan Technical College from the age of eleven to sixteen. This school was for those boys who barely passed the Eleven Plus entrance exam. Whereas those that passed it comfortably went to the grammar schools of West Monmouth or Abersychan and those who failed that exam went to Twmpath Secondary Modern school. So we boys at the Tech were considered to be of average intelligence and, therefore, we were being educated to be engineers that could be usefully employed by the local coal mines, steel works and factories. Like most boys, of that age, I was more interested in playing sports, walking the hills for exciting things to do or chasing girls. I spent very little of my out of school time applying myself to any school projects and because of this my grades suffered. It wasn't that I was dull, it was that as a naïve lad I could not grasp the importance of finishing school with good grades, at the age of sixteen, Back then I had an English Language teacher named Mr. Bees, who for obvious reasons was sarcastically known to us school boys as Buzzer. He was a crusty old guy with scary piercing eyes and looking back, at that time, he could not have been very far from retirement age. One day, in my final year, after marking our essays from the previous day's assignment, he handed them back to each boy and as he gave mine to me he made a point of singling me out. For about five full minutes he berated me, in front of the whole class, and announced in no uncertain words that taking the up-coming end of year exams was for me a complete waste of time.

I was totally embarrassed by this turn of events and left the class with my head hung low with shame. I was infuriated by this treatment and vowed that I would show that cantankerous old buzzard that he was completely wrong. For the next two months leading up to the exams I studied furiously at night and even early in the mornings, before leaving for school, which was totally unheard of where I was. concerned. The exams took place one per day, over a period of two weeks, and as soon as one was over I did intensive revision studies for the next one to take place the following day. When the results came out in the local newspaper my name was listed as having passed six, out of the eight taken, with flying colors. We seniors had two weeks left before the end of the school year and so we pretty much lolled around until our school days were no more. I was leaving his class room, on one of those days, when Buzzer singled me out and asked for me to remain behind after class. When everyone else had left the room he closed the door and turned to me and simply said"I knew that you could do it"This brought a lump to my throat because I suddenly realized that his outburst, when belittling me, was just his desperate way of giving me a quick kick in the rump. His wakeup call was the foundation for everything that I have achieved in my life ever since. That crafty old coot had seen something in me that I had not recognized in myself and I consider, that because of him, I have been fortunate enough to have had a great life. Mr Bees, I know that you are up there somewhere watching over me and from the bottom of my heart, I thank you.

The Long and Winding Road

My first wife was English and she gave me two great children Louise, who lives in Read, Lancashire and Richard, who lives in Tick Hill, Yorkshire, both in England. When they were around the age of sixteen I sat them down and, in that old Dickensian style, I told them to get their acts together because when they leave High Scool, at the age of eighteen, they would both be required to make their own way in life. This meant leaving home to begin their own adult lives because I did the same thing and it is the most positive way for children to grow into productive adults. It didn't really matter if they went to college, join the armed forces or become a skilled craftsman so long as it made them a person of independent means. The reason for this drastic edict was to teach them not to expect to stay at home and do nothing as so many other kids choose to do. As you are well aware, by now, I left home at the age of nineteen and on looking back this choice was the making of me as an independent man. Well my ultimatum worked too well and over the years I have become to realise that I basically shot myself in the foot. My children are so independent that they both live three thousand miles away from me and I only see them about once a year. I have been hoisted on my own pettard but I must say that inspite of this undesirable affect, I am immensely proud of what they have both achieved. My daughter has even given me a grandson, Jack, who is also turning out to be quite a special young man. My son has given one hundred percent to everything that he has been involved with and this also makes me extremely proud

When Louise and Richard were born I was twenty six and twenty eight years of age respectively I was unable to attend their births because they were both born Caesarian style. I was at the hospital for the duration of their births but I was not allowed in the operating theatre. Some years later my first marriage broke up, mainly because of my own selfish needs, and the second woman in my life was American. Although we lived together for seventeen years, up until she died, we were never married as we both preferred it that way. In 1983, when I was forty three years old, my fiance went into labor with our daughter whose name was Megan Lynn. She was born extremely premature and I am afraid that she was too small and destined not to live long after birth. Because of this and the fact that her mother was to deliver her in the natural manner, this time I was present at the birth.

The reason that I am writing about this event at all is that I was so amazed by the courage that a woman shows during child birth. A man will never fully appreciate what a woman is all about until he has witnessed this event. At what could possibly be described as the worst time of their lives, they are at their most magnificent. A man can never fully understand what a woman actually is until he has seen the agony that they go through to keep our world populated. Any man, who takes his woman for granted, should be made to sit through a natural child birth so that he can have an attitude adjustment and realize why women are so necessary to our human race. Without their supreme sacrifices and hardships life, as we know it, would ebb away and the likes of us would disappear. So gentlemen, and I use the term loosely, straighten up and fly right and do not take for granted our partners in procreation as the alternative to this situation could be the extinction of the human race. That is my lecture and sermon all rolled into one. Amen.

Seven
Crazier Than Fiction

Some things that have happened, during my life, are worth remembering for other than the normally accepted reasons. Some of them even border on the sublime and even the ridiculous because of their most unusual of circumstances. Never the less, these farcical pieces of Tom foolery have become almost typical of what can happened to me, throughout my life, to makes it far from normal. For instance on one hot, sultry evening my wife Sharon and I were sitting out on our front porch having a cocktail each and listening to the frogs croaking out their serenade. One of the croaked melodies seemed to be quite near to us and after sitting there for a while and pondering this highly intelligent phenomenon, Sharon espied the rogue frog perched up on our porch light next to the front door.

The frog was one of those bulging eyed almost albino looking tree types which have those suction cups on their feet which allows them to climb vertical walls. This was obviously how he found his way up to the top of our porch light which, incidentally, has a pagoda shaped lid on the top. It is quite rare to be able to see this type of frog, up close and personal, and so I decided to inspect it at a shorter range. I stood up and walked over to the porch light and was but a mere foot or two away from it. As I stood there observing this cute little critter, which by this time had ceased to croak, the most unexpected event took place much to my chagrin. For some inexplicable reason the frog, who up to this point had not batted an eye lid, decided to leap off the porch light. Not only was this a hugh suprize to me it was also most discerting as the air bourne frog landed right on my head. With a feeling of both surprize and discomfort I started to dance around the front porch like a screaming Watusi warrior. This was received with much delight by Sharon who was, by this time, laughing uncontrollably with delight. That damn tree frog, with its suction cupped feet, would not let go of my head and held on for the ride which must have been quite exciting for him. Finally, after what seemed like an eternity to me, he dismounted from my head and flew off into the night never to be seen or heard of again. I am sure that this entire episode only took about three minutes but it is three minutes of my life that I would gladly forfiet.

Well, the whole ludicrous incident made Sharon's night and this story is frequently rolled out at various social gatherings for the entertainment of all and sundry. Lets face it, it is the little things in life, such as this, that helps us to forget all the other more tedious elements that drive us insane with boredom. It is the joy of such times that holds our sorrows at bay. It is also moments like this that strip away the veneer of thousands of years of civilized mankind as back to the jungle we go in less than a heart beat. A little two year old girl that I know, named Marina, had a similar incident when, against the advise of her mother, she tried to kiss one of the many small lizard that are frequently found here about. The hapless lizard clamped onto her lower lip and would not let go even though she danced around in a similar manner to my previously described gyrations. The lizard did eventually let go and I suspect that after this occurrence she might want to forego the rigors of trying to find a hansom one.

The Long and Winding Road

Right now, as I sit here typing, we have yet another unusual situation going on in our bathroom. My wife arose to visit there, a week ago, then shouted for me to come immediately as there was a strange sight to be seen. I walked in to witness a cute little frog in the bathroom hand basin. His head was sticking out of the overflow outlet hole and how, in God's green acre, he got there is a complete mystery. It is very unlikely that he hopped in through the front door and decided to go into the bathroom, climb up to the hand basin and make his home there. The only explanation that we can come up with is that he must have been living in a large calla lily plant which was gifted to us, by a visiting house guest. She bought it at an outdoor garden nursery and when she brought it home we put, this three foot tall potted plant, just a few feet away from the bathroom door. That was about six weeks prior to our first sighting, of this uninvited visitor, which really is a bizarre situation even for Florida where we frequently encounter a good amount of God's creatures.

Perhaps, after his stay on the plant, he felt that it was now time to move on to bigger and better things which precipitated his sudden appearance. With his head poking out of the over flow outlet it appears that he has found his new home which is testimony to the fact that he has moved out into the big world. I made several attempts to extricate him but every time I reached to get him, he retreated back into the outlet hole. It's a little weird sharing your wash basin with another creature but if he wants to hang out and watch us clean our teeth and wash our hands, so be it. I hope that he will decide to move on soon because I refuse to hire a critter catcher to alleviate such a small intruder.

Living in the semi tropics, such as this, is full of unexpected incidents and to occasionally find a small gecko type lizard, in the house, is quite usual and perfectly acceptable because they also feed on small insects. I remember, from my past visits to Italy, that they also have this occurrence and the Italians call them "fortunatos" as it is considered to bring good luck to the household which they inhabit. You might be wondering why I would even mention such a trivial incident but this is just another example of how Mother Nature will interact, with us human beings, in the most unexpected ways here in the subtropics where we are fortunate enough to live. She never ceases to surprise and amaze but I do hope that Mr. Froggy has not come-a-courting because Sharon is becoming quite enamored with him.

Similarly, the other evening we had yet another equally bizarre occurrence. As if playing tricks on us, Mother Nature introduced us to yet another one of her more unique creatures. On these beautiful summer nights we are in the habit of leaving our front door completely wide open to enjoy the cool evening breeze. All of a sudden my wife noticed that we were not entirely alone. Hanging from the living room ceiling was, what at first appeared to be, a bat but on closer inspection we could see that it was, in fact, a large moth. It was indeed the size of a bat which just about confirmed that it was the largest moth that we had ever encountered. It was a monster moth measuring approximately nine inches from wing tip to wing tip and it was a gorgeous dark brownish/maroon in color.. Since my wife does not like things that flitter around the house by night, it was my task to catch the wee beastie and return it back outside. Trying to capture this lovely creature, without damaging its wings, was no mean task but finally I managed to usher it out through the front door which my wife eagerly slammed shut. The moth disappeared off into the night, never to be seen again, which is a pity because I will now have difficulty persuading others as to the authenticity of its size. We did take a photograph of it, on our cell phone, however and alas we had nothing next to it that would gage its true proportions. Explaining this to other people is akin to a fisherman relating his story about the one that got away. I can garauntee that very few people will believe a story about a moth with a nine inch wing span. Such was its magnitude it could be considered by the military in covert operations. They could strap a camera to it and, as a drone, it could be used to spy on our country's enemies. They would never suspect such skullduggery from this frail and innocent creature. What a boundless thing a rampant imagination can be.

On a separate occasion yet another toe curling, butt clenching event happened, in the confines of my island home. My wife and I were preparing to go to bed one evening. when I remembered that I had left our garage door opened and so I stepped into the pitch black garage to rectify the afore mentioned misdeed. We have since removed that garage door and replaced it with a sliding glass door wall. The old garage door was one of those up and over roller designs and so all I had to do was grab it and pull down for it to roll into a closed position. As I stood there in the dark, to began this simple chore, I thought that I felt something touch the back of my neck which made me pause for a moment.. As I proceeded to pulled down, with one last energetic tug, something wrapped itself aroud my head and I immediately was propelled into one of those previously mentioned African tribal Watusi dances.

The more that I spun around the more the poltegeist wrapped around my head and I was, by now, fighting with it on the floor. At this point Sharon entered the garage, to check on all the noises and commotion. She switched on the garage light to find me furiously wrestling with a shirt. Apparently she had, earlier that evening, hung a shirt up to dry on the rear end of the garage mechanism. As I pulled the garage door down the mechanism, and the shirt hanging from it, was propelled towards my back until the last door tug wrapped the shirt around me and the fight was on. Once again my wife, God bless her soul, was full of wonderment as to how a fairly well educated guy, such as me, could end up in such dire straights. My only answer to this conundrum is that it is the unknown and the unexpected in life that can turn a level headed man into a quivering, bumbling idiot. As before Sharon cannot wait to roll out these quirky and somewhat embarrassing anecdotes at each and every opportunity.

I try never to miss an opportunity to bring levity and amusement, into the lives of less fortunate people. This is one of my primary joys in life and, to this end, there are no occasions too austere or formal to escape my indulgence. Some of my simple yet riveting statements such as"Are you dying to try it, or trying to diet?"to an oversized person or"Happy have-a nursery"to a pregnant woman, is all part of my witty repertoire. If I join a group of people already deep in conversation I will ask if I am protruding, instead of intruding. This unsuspecting comment usually lets me directly into the conversation because, as I am sure you are aware, the meaning of protruding comes from a whole different ball game if you'll excuse the obvious pun. My wit is as subtle as a sledge hammer which I wield with deft precision. I was told once, at some stuffy social gathering, that there was no drinking allowed to which I replied that, therefore, I would drink quietly. Because I do believe that pandemonium is caused by pandas, this type of word misrepresentation is grist for the mill of contradiction and should always be taken advantage of. Comments, such as these, are all that it takes for me to realize that the age old adage of"Speak and not just talk"has been well applied. Lord Byron, I am sure, would be impressed but Lord Tennyson, on the other hand, would pitch a fit.

There is a wild man loose, on this island where I live, who can pack more enjoyment into any given weekend than anyone else that I have ever met. His name is Darrin Wash and although he is a builder by trade, during the week, he is a party animal as soon as five o'clock on Friday rolls around. I play soccer twice a week with Darrin as we are both part of the"crazy gang"who play year round up at Holmes Beach in ninety degrees plus heat. Darrin goes missing quite often on the weekends when he learns that some rock band or other is playing within a two hundred mile radius of where he lives. At the drop of a hat he just jumps on his Harley Davison motorbike and zooms off into the distance like the Lone Ranger of Anna Maria Island. Darrin also throws probably the best parties that it has been my pleasure to attend and he has his own in-house music studio where he plays drums and where he invites anyone with any musical ability to sit in for an improvised jam session.

I mention all this about Darrin because he got me tanked up on some wild arsed Nova Scotia brand of beer at such a party one night. Afterwards I went home and somehow fell down, out on my front porch, and I re-injured my right shoulder. Both of my shoulders have been dislocated from way back in my rugby playing days and it doesn't take too much for them to pop out of joint. I did not go to the hospital and luckily for me, after two days of agony, I rolled over in bed and, crack, the shoulder popped right back in place. After that my shoulder ached for about a month and I still had to carry on playing soccer in the Anna Maria Community Center in-house recreation league. I was rather afraid that if I was to collide with someone, on the field of battle, my shoulder might pop out again and so I needed to add some padding underneath my soccer shirt to afford me some protection. I tried all sorts of things but none of them worked because they would not stay in place, on my shoulders, while I was running around on the field of play. I needed padding with some adhesive attached so that they would stay in place during the rough and tumble of the game. At this point my wife, being her father's daughter and never short of ideas, came up with a masterful plan, She attached two Maxi pads, one on each shoulder to the inside of my shirt, and"I'll be a son of a gun"it worked perfectly. Now this ploy was a closely guarded secret until we were all in Slim's Bar after one of the games and my wife, to get her jollies, decided to reveal our master plan. Well you can imagine the ribbing that I had to endure after this little gem of information was released to all and sundry. I am probably one of an elite band of men who can categorically give a glowing endorsement for that wonderful brand of feminine hygiene products.

So alert the media as this story has just gone ballistic what with all the modern day electronic message gadgets. Even some jolly swag man, camped by a billabong in central Australia, can get a good chuckle out of this one. It could even make the Guinness Book of World Records because I don't thing that any other man, in his right mind, would openly admit to such an absurd story such as this. So thank you Darrin Wash for being the unwitting architect of this bizarre incident and perhaps, one day soon, I can return the favor with interest. So, Mr. Wash, keep your musket loaded and your powder dry because pay backs are a bitch.

On a recent trip, from Florida to a book signing in Cleveland, Ohio, my wife and I stopped over for the night near a small town in South Carolina called Rock Hill. The motel that we stopped at for the night, just south of the border with North Carolina, was as rural as it could possibly be. After checking in to our room and freshening up we inquired, at the front desk, if there was a restaurant nearby where we could get a good meal. On arriving at the recommended eatery we scanned the menu for a hearty meal which we desperately needed after spending around ten hours in the car that day. A waitress approached our table to inquire if we would like a beverage to which I requested a beer. At this the young waitress burst into guffaws of laughter and said that I always asked for beer every time I visited her diner. This was news to me because not only had I never set foot inside that establishment before, I had never even been within about three hundred miles of that particular location.

Anyway, they did not serve alcohol and so I let that one slide and continued to peruse the menu when, lo and behold, listed on the menu was a number of meals featuring quail. Now the only time that I have ever seen this sweet little bird featured on a menu has been in Ritzy cafes in such cities as Paris, London and Rome and so to see it at this outpost of civilization was a total shock. Suspecting that our young waitress was a good target for some fun I decided to ramp up the excitement a few notches. I beckoned her over and with a straight face I pretended not to know what a quail was. She said that it was a bird and so I then asked if it was as large as an ostrich or as small as a parrot which set her off again, with shrieks of laughter, as she went back into the kitchen all aquiver. On the menu was a meal of quail with eggs and so the next time she dared to approach our table I asked her if the eggs came inside the quail at which point she totally lost it and retreated from our presence never to be seen again. I believe that she was afraid to come out of the kitchen because another waitress came over to take our order. By this time all the customers at this small diner were enjoying the cabaret which seemed to put everyone in a pleasant mood. As we departed quite a few of the beaming locals wished us bon voyage and wave goodbye to us with the fervent hope that we would pass that way again in the not too distant future. Once again my quirky sense of humor had amused a place full of strangers and, as I have been told before, once seen never forgotten. I was once asked to come forth but unfortunately I came fifth and lost the bet.

Around five months after writing about me dislocating my shoulder, inadvertantly caused by Darrin Wash, justice was finally served when he too was aflicted with the exact same injury. Alcohol and skull duggery accompanieed this tragic incident but my voodoo curse finally took hold. Call it kismet or karma but it just goes to show that what goes around realy does come back around. In all fairness to Darrin he took it like a real trooper and two days after the event he turned up and played in an Island Rowdies pickup soccer game with his right arm craddled in a sling. My admiration for his tenacity was raised even more by this singular act of bravery tinged with a small amount of lunacy. This elevates him to being among a rare breed of Island soccer fanatics and this typifies why our group of reprobates is known as the Crazy Gang.

Eight
De Ja Vu
All Over Again

I was in Wales on one of my annual trips and was doing a book signing at a W. H. Smith's book store in Cwmbran, a town about four miles south of my home town of Pontypool. I really enjoy this type of event because it is a great opportunity for me to meet people that I have not seen in many a year. I always advertise these events, in the local newspapers, to let people know that I am around, in the hope that they will drop by for a chat and perhaps buy one of my books. I have been able to meet old friends, neighbors, sports acquaintances, work mates and even the occasional girl friend. Health wise some are in fairly good shape while others, alas, are suffering from all sorts of afflictions. One woman, named Joan, had not seen me since I was fourteen years of age when I was a Boy Scout and camped in the field next to her house in Mamhilled and survived on corned beef right out of the can. It was nice to get reacquainted with her and we shared some long forgotten stories of our misspent youth. She very kindly gave me a photo of the two of us, back then, to mark that auspicious occasion.

My good old pal Billy Sims, who lived in Edwards Street opposite my Grandma, always tracks me down. It is reassuring to find that some people can remember me, from days gone by, when I was young and full of promise. Some people back home say that I have hardly changed, apart from the gray hair, and that they instantly recognized me. One smiling young lady walked up to me and told me that she had been to Anna Maria Island, where I currently live, and that she and her husband even had cocktails at my house. This event escaped my recollection until she related it with more of the details and jogged into gear my cluttered memory. Apparently, this young couple were good friends, back in Wales, with my long time friend Geoff West and his wife Vicky.

I also remember doing a book signing at another W. H. Smith book store in the town of Newport and I was thinking that business was not as brisk as it had been on previous years. A short time later I found out that the famous Welsh world champion boxer Joe Calzaghe was signing his book just a few doors away at Waterstone's book store. I guess his book"No Ordinary Joe"was a big success and somewhat over shadowed my meager offerings. The thought crossed my mind that I should walk over and have a word with him about his untimely interference but had immediate second thoughts as, after all, he was the undisputed middle weight champion of the world. One fierce stare from him would have been enough to knock me over and so, I took the"wait and watch"approach which I considered to be my best option. I figured that the old western movie ultimatum of "This town ain't big enough for the both of us"ploy, would be nothing short of a suicidal disaster. Joe, incidentally, has now retired from the boxing ring after a glowing career of almost five years as being the best fighter, at his weight, and the whole of Wales is justifiably proud of him. From his little boxing club, in Newbridge, he traveled the world taking on all-comers, while dishing out some severe beatings and emerged triumphantly.

On a more recent visit to South Wales I was staying in Caerleon, the most obvious site of the fabled Camelot. One morning my wife and I stopped in at The Frwm, one of that town's more famous cafes, for our morning cups of coffee. The café was quite empty and so I could not help but notice that one of the other customers, an attractive woman, was paying more than average interest to our presence. Every time that I would glance in her direction I found her staring intently at our every movement This in itself is not too unusual because my wife is an attractive woman and I, if I may be so bold, cut a fine figure of a man. As time went on the woman seemed more familiar to me and then all of a sudden I realized who she was. She just so happen to be the very last young girl that I dated immediately prior to my leaving home to work in England. Because of my monumental decision to leave Wales I had left her in the lurch and she became a casualty of circumstances beyond her control. To say that she was collateral damage would be harsh but in those days when I made a decision I would move on and never look back. I did not indicate that I recognized her, to either my wife or to the long lost girl friend, as I thought this to be improper. This is just another example of how my past keeps coming back to haunt me.

At that moment my life had completed a full circle and brought me face to face with my youthful past, yet luckily for me there was no retribution. I know that woman recognized me for who I was but she decided not to confront me over the consequences of my departure. She eventually stood up, paid her bill, gather her purse and classily exited the building with one last glance back from the door in my direction. This accentuated the fact that she had recognized who I was and she showed a great deal of restraint and a modicum of class giving on her part. I was somewhat relieved because some women have long memories and so you had best know not to disturb the beast from within and, no pun intended, let sleeping dogs lie low.

On last years trip to Sharon's family in Michigan we decided that because we were members of our Moose Lodge, directly adjacent to the beach in Bradenton Beach, that we would try to visit a Moose Lodge while up in the Detroit area. Although we were staying with Sharon's family, out on the south west side of that region, we would be traveling about and so if we happened upon a Lodge we would barge right on in. On one of the days, a Thursday I believe, we were driving through Westland and there, right near the traffic lights at Newburg and Ford Road, was just what we had hoped for. We turned the car around and went back for a look see. There wasn't much going on but we were warmly welcomed and we were told about a party that they would be having the following Sunday afternoon. The party was for the birthday of one of their staunch members and the highlight was entertainment by a Patsy Cline look alike singer. Well Sharon and I just love Patsy Cline's music and so we vowed to come back for the festiveties.

Although we were quite busy we were able to make it to their party and the food and entertainment was first class. It was a hot summer's day and all the tables were set up outside in the courtyard area. As we were mixing and mingling with the crowd. I was talking to one of the members when I noticed, across the other side of the gathering, a guy who was waving in our direction. At this point I informed my companion that someone was trying to attract his attention. He went over and spoke to the waving guy and then came back and said that the guy was, in fact, trying to get my attention. I went over to him and it turned out to be Bob Miran who I knew from when I attended the Canadian Legion Club, before I left for Florida, some thirteen years earlier. He said that he recognized me the moment that I came in and that he was shocked to see me in there. He had been a member of long standing at this Moose Lodge and never considered that he would ever see me again in his lifetime. We reminisced about the"good old days"when, as younger men, we though that the world was our oyster and that health problems and monies were never an issue.

It was great to see him and his wife after all those years. His wife was the daughter of a good friend of mine, a Scottish guy named Andy Roberts. Andy was in fact the Chaplain at the Canadian Legion Post and was instrumental in initiating a swear box in an attempt to curb the outbursts of profane language. Because of this singular piece of ingenuity he and I were closely connected, for all the wrong reasons, as I was a frequent donator to that noble cause. I also remember that. as Legion Chaplain, Andy had to recite the Soldiers Prayer at the Memorial Day celebration but with his strong Scottish brogue no-one could understand a single word that he spoke. Playing pool for money against him and his Scottish compatriot Billy Cameron was like trying to get blood from a stone but what good hearted people they were. Unfortunately since I moved from that area both Billy and Andy have passed away but I sent on my best wishes to Andy's widow, Etta. What a blast from the past and it surely proves, in my case, the saying that a bad penny will inevitably show up sooner or later.

Here on our island there is a music festival, up at Holmes Beach park, on the last Friday of every month. There is no entrance fee and there are a goodly few booths selling all kinds of art, clothing, local souvreneres, foods and of course the obligatory beer concession tent. Some people just come to show off their dogs, all decked out in their dogie attire, and the human attendees have a good time also. There is always two or three local live bands playing music and the indulgence of booze will always urge people to dance. A few months ago, towards the end of the evening, my wife and I were talking to a group of soccer playing buddies at the spot where they always congrugate, the beer tent of course. Sharon and I were just making moves to leave when up came three women, all dressed alike. They were wearing tweed like capes, which is completely out of fashion in Florida, and I made the comment to them that they looked as if they had just attended a Harry Potter convention. As they were standing near by one of them turned to me and said"Why do you seem so familiar to me ?"to which I replied that I had absolutely no idea. When she heard my voice I saw the expression on her face change as she stared at me with a shocked appearance. She turned to her two friends and was pointing at me while she whispered her revelation to them at which juncture they all turned and stared at me with mouths agape.

Sharon and I left at this juncture because she had to open Paradise Café at 6:30AM the following morning and it was a further two days later that the light bulb flashed on and I remembered who that woman was. She was the first woman that I made friends with when I first came to America and that was back in 1976. We met in an Irish bar, named The Dublin Inn, down on Schaefer Road in East Dearborn. She was a Buyer at the Ford Motor Company's head office and I was a salesman who was calling on that company to sell my product line. As a buyer she was not dealing with the product that I sold but I knew that Ford had the policy of periodically rotating their buyers to give them experience with a greater variety of products. My thought was that, with any amount of luck, one day perhaps she would be sitting at a desk where the orders for my product line would land. If this should ever happen she would be an extremely influential person for me to know and, therefore, it was in my best interest to keep that avenue of opportunity open. To this end I would meet her for a drink or two on occasions but I had to discontinue this when I realized that she had strong feelings for me and I was married to my first wife at the time. Although my family was still back in England and had not joined me in America yet, I did not want any complications when they finally arrived in the States.

I bumped into her, by accident, several years later and she still had the hots for me and so I decided that it would be wise to gracefully back away and not stir up her smoldering emotions. As everyone knows"Hell hath no fury like a woman scorned". However, I must admit that she is still a cute little lady but I have since moved on with my life and am now married to a beautiful woman who I adore. Never-the-less seeing her again brought back floods of memories from some thirty plus years ago. This was such an exciting period in my life, what with being in this strange new land called America. Winston Churchill summed it up perfectly when he once said that Britain and the USA were two countries divided by a common language This incredible event had occurred twelve hundred miles away and thirty five years after the original incidental location.

This meeting was more like a ghost from the past event more so than a blast from the past. It seems that I am destined to be part of a select group of people who within their lifetimes seem to experience, at regular intervals, such unique encounters of an strange kind. After relating some of my odd experiences of the strange kind one guy, who I met at a Welsh Convention, was convinced that I possessed some Bardic super natural powers. He has contacted me on several occasions and has asked me to consider returning to Wales with him for an investigation of the true locations of Camelot and King Arthur's grave. Although it is true that I do experience some unusual and unexplained incidents and situations this is stretching things to the absolute extreme of the imagination.

Another curiously strange event happened a few years ago while, here in Florida, I was watching a Red Wings ice hockey game live on the television from the Joe Louis Arena in Detroit. There was a lull in the action on the ice and, as is the usual routine, the cameraman at the game began to pan around the crowded seats until play was resumed. Would you believe it, the camera focused in on one particular attendee and when I took note I was looking a past girl friend of mine from about fifteen years previous. She did not seem to be aware that the camera was on her because she didn't jump up and give the usual wave to the camera. She was, in fact, chatting to some of the other Red

Wings fans sitting nearby and was oblivious of the fact that she was being shown live on a national television channel. The game, that night, was a Stanley Cup play-off match and the arena was filled to capacity and so for the camera man to pick her out of that capacity crowd was a long shot at best. This particular woman was a red hot Wings fan and for her to be at this prestigious game was no surprise to me. However, for me to be sitting in front of my television at home in Florida and to be looking at her, all the way up there in Michigan, was a complete shock to me. It was not quite the same as meeting her face to face, never the less, the whole incident was quite eerie and unnerving. Yet on the other hand, it was unexpectedly pleasant and it was gratifying to see that her life is still full of excitement and that she still enjoys her passion for the Detroit Red Wings.

Sharon and pal hamming it up.

Lyn and crazy Hugh Lyndsay share a joke.

John Lennon's original stand-up piano.

Lyn and Sharon with Brenda and the late Howard Marley.

Nine
The Milk of
Human Kindnesss

My life has been blessed as I now live in the Garden of Eden here on Anna Maria Island. It is so beautiful and breath taking that each day I thank my lucky stars that I stumbled upon this Paradise on Earth. Because of this I am in the habit, as most residents are, of picking up any trash items that would detract from this idyllic setting. As I walk the beaches and nature trails I pick up any paper, plastic or metal debris that I come across along the way. Not only are these items unsightly but they can also be dangerous and sometimes deadly to our local wild life. It is in everyone's interest to keep our island as pristine as possible to the mutual benefit of both humans and wild life alike. Visitors to our island must be aware of the dire consequences of not heeding this unwritten rule.

With this in mind I was returning from the beach recently when I came across an unusually large pile of plastic shopping bags which had been left under a palm tree just to the side of the beach access path. At first I was naturally annoyed at this thoughtless action but as I investigated the problem it became immediately clear that this was not a random act of littering. It became apparent to me that held inside this pile of tattered bags was, what looked like, someone's last worldly possessions.

The bags contained an amount of clothing, some food, an assortment of reading material, a few personal hygiene products and a variety of paper products. Recently I heard a statement which predicted that a large number of people, throughout America, were just two pay checks away from living in a cardboard box. As I stared at this collection of items the cold, hard fact of what I was looking at became chillingly obvious. These were, in fact, the contents of a person's life which had, for what ever reason, hit rock bottom and had consequently rendered the owner homeless. Due to this revelation I decided to leave the pile remain there but for seven consecutive days I return to monitor any progress but, alas, there was none.

Because of our ideal weather conditions, here in Florida, it is a magnet for homeless people who would prefer not to tolerate the rigors of an extremely cold winter up in the northern States. Rather than sleep outside in sub zero temperatures they come down here but even our winter nights can be less that comfortable while living alfresco. The main stumbling block to this is that here on our island we have no charitable organizations, such as the Salvation Army, who can offer a warm bed and a hot meal for these unfortunate people. This means that if they are found by the local police they will be transported to the main land where these facilities, do exist and if no available accommodation exists there, they will be carted off to the County Jail.

This, in itself, is an act of kindness but I am told that when people are homeless this action also prevents them from becoming involved in petty stealing, shop lifting and house or vehicle robberies. In other words it takes temptation away and leaves our community in complete harmony. Not all homeless people are penniless and some might even have a small monthly income such as a veteran's pension, however, this only allows them to barely exist without being able to afford a roof over their heads. Therefore on this somewhat remote island, without any social service amenities if a person opts to winter out the weather here they had better have a contingency plan, on which to survive, as man cannot live on bread alone.

On the eighth day I am once again staring into these tattered plastic bags which had not been retrieved by their owner and which by now are damp, dirty and beginning to get moldy. My thought now is that the owner has been unavoidably detained, perhaps by the police, and therefore it is time for these items to be removed. I was intrigued by this circumstance and so before throwing them into the garbage I took them to my yard and emptied out all the items for inspection. If ever there was an inside view into what being homeless is all about then this was it. All the bare facts were revealed which gave an amazing insight into the minimum needs, for survival under the stars, when the night temperatures drop to around fifty or even forty degrees Fahrenheit.

In the clothing category there were but four items. One, a hooded fleece lined sweat top which happened to be a man's extra large size and had an Anna Maria Island. logo embroider on the front and appeared to be a recent acquisition. This item would be ideal for when the temperature drops uncomfortably low. Two,was a flannel sheet which I can imagine was useful to wrap around a person's body for that extra bit of warmth when sleeping. Another piece of apparel was a well worn pair of flip-flops which would lead me to believe that the owner must have had a second, hopefully more sturdy, pair of footwear currently on his feet. The last item was a colorful beach sized towel which, as well as for the obvious, could be used for extra bedding warmth.

The food was equally as sparse and could hardly be called mouth watering. The first item was a plastic zip locked bag of sun flower seeds which a person, under normal circumstances, would use for an in between meal snack. These usually come under the banner of health foods but of hardly any nutritional value. The second item was a half eaten bag of roasted peanuts, still in their shells, which again would have limited affects to fend off the gnawing pangs of hunger. The third item was a large plastic bottle of water which would have been essential for drinking and possibly for cleaning one's teeth. The fourth item was a single can of Chef Boyardee ravioli which is pasta and abounds with carbohydrates but not so good when eaten cold. Unfortunately, the can had early signs of rust on it and looked old which might have rendered it unfit for human consumption anyway. There was also a small bag with an assortment of various fast food condiments, most likely collected from the occasions when a small amount of money afforded this person a cheap meal at a fast food outlet.

In a separate bag was an assortment of pulp fiction paper back books which I am sure would be useful to wile away many an idle hour. One in particular which caught my eye was a book of short Alfred Hitchcock stories which somewhat proved that not only could this person read but he also had a discerning taste in literature. Surprisingly there was also several editions of the National Geographic magazines which again underlined that this person might have a reasonable amount of education. There was also a ream of brown paper towels and white restaurant styled napkins which I am sure had an abundance of uses for a person in these circumstances. In an even smaller plastic bag was a few toiletry items which included a man's styled shaving razor, an unopened bottle of body wash and a small deodorant applicator. I did not find any sun block products but I am sure that, if this season was in the summer months, such an item would have been essential. After duly making a mental note of these belongings I condemned them to the garbage as would the city authorities, sooner or later, when they came across them.

What happened to this individual I do not know nor where and why he, as I assumed the person to be, was being detained is an equal mystery. All this occurred during the two weeks leading up to Christmas, in the year of our Lord 2011, when far too many people were literally fighting over gifts at the mall. I am not a deeply religious person but I do have a conscience and I ask myself what happened to"Good will to all men"as practiced by the good Samaritan. A simple gesture such as a few dollars, a cup of coffee or a bite to eat could mean so much to a displaced person. It is far too easy for the majority of us to pass judgment on those less fortunate than ourselves. Some of these people were once proud and honorable human beings who somehow, not necessarily through any fault of there own, have slid down the slippery slopes of despair. In these uncertain economic times I hope that none of us ever experience the indignity of home-lessness. Let us make amends and do something for the good of others and hope, upon hope, that we never find ourselves in this unenviable of all positions.

Since setting out to tell this particular story, several months ago, I was not aware that I would become personally involved with this subject. A young man, who I know through play-ing soccer, has found himself in this horrendous situation. His mother, for some unknown reason, decided to move back to her home state of Minnesota but this poor boy decided to stay here and live as a homeless person. This is a devastating posi-tion to be in particularly since the young man in question suffers from schizophrenia. Perhaps this affliction was the source that prompted him to make this earth shattering decision. I bump into him from time to time and I have become in the habit of giving him some money, food or drinks so that he can survive at subsistence level. I can only assume that he cannot afford to take his medication which helps to keep him on a mental even keel.. All this plus sleeping at night on the beach can only make his situation worse and I hope and pray that someone, in his family, will reconnect with him and give him the help that he so desperately needs. Once this phenomenon directly affects some-one that you personally know the implications become all too real. It puts a recognizable face to a growing problem and you had better hope that this ugly problem does not visit itself at your door. In the mean time all I can do is to ensure that he has a few creature comforts to help him through each and every one of his tedious days.

Ten
Flip Flops And Tank Tops

On the bright side, of the equation, living on this Gulf of Mexico island is just about as perfect as it can get. Down here the people wear bright colored clothes have beaming smiles and are full of the joys of life. The island is split into the three small towns of Bradenton Beach, Holmes Beach and Anna Maria from which the island's name was derived. There are only about ten thousand people that are permanent residence of this island and I am proud to be one. However for most of the year the population doubles with visitors from Britain, Europe and other parts of South America. Then through the months of November, to the end of April, the population is quadrupled when the"snow birds,"as we call them, come swarming down from Canada and all of those cold and frost covered States up in the north.

We only have one main road, the Gulf of Mexico Drive, which travels north and south up and down the eight mile long island and so the influx of all these tourists causes a logistical problem. However, the money that they all spend here, is a huge boost to our island economy. The shops, the restaurants and the beaches are full of happy people making hay while the sun shines. It is a joy to my soul to mix, on a daily basis, with so many sun tanned, happy people. Because of the wonderful climate here I see more shapely, bikini clad maidens who can only be rivaled by their counterparts on the French or Italian Riviera. I do believe that living in this stress free environment has, I am sure, added five more years to the end of my life's span. Enjoying the company of some reasonable rich and famous folk, on a daily basis, is spiritually uplifting. All these assets mixed with the continual pleasure of the exotic flora and fauna,of this sub tropical enclave, brings joy to my heart.

Just the other day my wife and I were driving off the island to run some errands. As we crossed the Manatee draw bridge, onto the main land, we spotted a Bald Eagle perch on the bare limb of a tree. It was no more than thirty yards off the road and was probably eying the inter-costal waters for his morning snack. This might not sound like too much of an event but this majestic bird was near to extinction from the use of DDT as a crop pesticide spray. When the eagle ingested the DDT, through the food chain, it caused their egg shells to become so thin that they would prematurely break and the hatchling would die. By the time that this catastrophic occurrence was discovered the bald eagle population was down to a mere few thousand in the whole United States. Their numbers are now increasing again and to see this awe inspiring bird, so brazenly sitting without fear so near to human habitat, is an encouraging sign. This particular specimen stood about three and a half feet tall and as it finally flew away you could see that its wing span was between eight and nine feet across. To think that one of our early Presidents wanted to make the turkey America's national symbol. To give the turkey preference,over this majestic creature, is just ludicrous to say the least. This would be tantamount to a thimble, not a symbol, of that person's mistaken choice and a huge disgrace to the American race.

Driving south along Gulf Drive you will cross another draw bridge before arriving at the very wealthy community of Longboat Key. The speed limit there is 30 MPH but this gives the traveler ample time to view all the million dollar homes along the way. After crossing yet another draw bridge, at the southern end of Longboat Key, the tourist will soon be at Saint Armand's Circle. This is a superb area for browsing around the somewhat expensive shops and ethnic restaurants and for mixing with the hoi polloi who live there about. From there the inter coastal bay can be crossed, via a beautiful new arched bridge, to enter down town Sarasota which is a ritzy enclave for the retired rich from those northern bastions of industry. Still heading south down Highway 41, also known as the Tamiami Trail [because it was the original road that linked Tampa to Miami] the third of our Gulf islands can be found. This is named Siesta Key and it has a beach that has been voted the second best in the United States, only to be topped by a beach in Hawaii. The sand here is almost as fine as talcum powder and the ocean is as clear as crystal.

On Siesta Key every Sunday evenings, from around two hours before sunset, people begin to congregate to observe the totally free now famous Drum Circle. Everyone is welcome to join in regardless of age, sex or religion, as all that is required is something to bang and something to bang it with. There are often jugglers, belly dancers and sword balancers to be seen, who originate from a local circus company, and there is an open invitation for, one and all, to join in and dance.. Children and grown ups, alike, lose their inhibitions and cut loose in gay abandon as they wait for the sun to set. The beat of the drums is both rhythmic and incessant and it becomes extremely hypnotic, for all concerned. They finally leave the beach fully invigorated and with sand between their toes and their spirits restored. If you are ever in the area this is a not to be missed "must see"event and is just a forty-five minute drive south from Anna Maria Island. This small stretch of coast line is one of the nicest part of Florida and the ocean front, from Anna Maria Island and all the way south to Naples, is truly remarkable. This is the nearest thing to Paradise that can ever be experienced in my lifetime and so, come on down, the water is just fine.

The flip flop culture can occasionally work against a person as I found out just a few months ago. My house stands on a two lot piece of land which is five thousand square feet in area. I have, on this property, around seventy to eighty shrubs, bushes and trees varying in height from around three feet tall all the way up to sixty feet. I love working in my yard and this is just as well because most every day I am out there fighting Mother Nature. In some ways it is a futile battle because She will always win but the vegetation is so colorful and so fragrant that, when it is properly tended to, it looks amazingly beautiful. The different colors of the flowers and bushes are so vivid and vibrant that it is a treat just to sit on the front porch and survey the scenery. The only thing that I don't do is cut my grass and, to this end, I employ a young Mexican man, named Jose, who does this for me by using just a Weed Wacker. The only part of my property that still has grass is the stretch across the front of the house. The grass used to go all the way around the house but slowly and gradually I have systematically laid down sea shells so that the grass will no longer grow on these parts.

The other day I was out around the back of the house and stepped off the path to retrieve some yard debris when I had a sudden agonizing sharp pain in my right foot. My first reaction was to make sure that I had not been stung or bitten by one of Florida's less beloved creatures but thank goodness this was not the case. I had, in fact, stepped onto a shelled area and a sharp tapered sea shell, called an auger, had penetrated clear through my flip flop which was a half of an inch thick. It then continued on through and stuck into the sole of my foot for a further half inch. I pulled it out immediately and came into the house and thoroughly cleaned the wound and then put iodine on to ensure that no germs were lingering within. I limped around for several weeks and had to pad, that area of my foot, so that I could continue to play in my weekly Soccer League. It just goes to show that it is unwise to drop ones guard for even a moment. Since we are below the frost line, down here in Florida, every precaution must be taken to immediately sterilize any wounds inflicted while working out in the soil, vegetation and particularly any bites, cuts or stings. About a year or two ago I cut my finger on a barnacle that was stuck to the bottom of a piece of boat deck which I salvaged from the sea. I did not properly clean that mere paper cut of a wound and I ended up having to go to the surgery for sixty consecutive days to have a one hour antibiotic drip put into my arm. That is no joke and should be drastically avoided at all costs.

When the tourist season is upon us I help out Sharon where she works at the Paradise Café. One of the many sumptuous meals on the menu is the tuna salad for which the owner, Jackie Estes, uses a complete can of the best albacore tuna which is considered to be the king of that species. One day a customer called me over and said that there was a foreign object in her tuna salad and when I examined the meal I found a sharks tooth lodged in the tuna. The boats that fish for tuna have a processing plant on board so that when they bring their catch into port the wholesaler has to just pay, load up and drive away with the catch. As this particular fish was being netted its thrashing about must have caught the attention of a shark who tried to get his share of the tuna. Well, all he got was a bite and that caused him to leave a souvenir tooth for the lucky customer. I also once saw a woman customer, at a different restaurant, pull a pearl out of a shell from her order of raw oysters. That trumps the sharks tooth event by a long shot, however, both are nice trinkets that can be hung on a chain around ones neck.

The beautiful weather is a huge factor as to why people live in Florida but this phenomenon is a two edged sword, Yes we do have, in the main, beautiful weather here but we also have, from time to time, hurricanes, tornadoes, violent tropical sea storms and even the annual forest fires. There is not a lot that we, on this island, can do about the tempests from the sea other than board up the house and hunker down with the hope that the wrath of nature will pass us by without adversely affecting our lives too much. Hurricanes can be massive, some the size of Texas, and these are capable of wiping from the face of the earth whole towns. The last major storm to hit my island was back in 1941 and, as good luck would have it, back then this island was sparsely populated. Although we all know that this situation is a craps shoot, we abide here with the hope that Mother Nature will look kindly upon us in these eventualities.

Tornadoes, another of life's unpredictable events, happens when the southern hot air mixes with the northern cold air while swirling in opposite directions. This then causes a wind funnel which rotates, as it moves along, with winds from seventy to one hundred and fifty miles per hour. This also can destroy towns but it is narrower in scope, than the hurricane, and has the odd affliction of destroying one house while leaving the house immediately next to it completely unharmed. Our tropical sea storms, on the western side of Florida, come from the Gulf of Mexico to our west and there is basically nothing that we can do about them as long as we stay on land. The fishermen, out of nearby Cortez, have to run for their lives and try not to get caught in heavy seas.. Incidentally, Cortez Village is the last operating fishery, of its kind, left in the whole State of Florida. The fishing boats can put in and unload, the already processed fish, right there at the dockside. Forest fires are abundant during the summer months and some are deliberately set, by the Forestry Department, to clear overgrown tracts of land. Some fires get out of hand and even burn down some houses on the odd occasion but in the main here on the island we are isolated, from these dangers. We have a half of a mile strip of water which protects us from the fury, that is fire, by impeding its progress. This is a great comfort to everyone who resides here on this small neck of land and has proved to be one of nature's blessing in disguise.

Florida is famous for having the most thunder and lightning storms in the whole of America and some of these are awesome to behold. A few months ago I was playing in a quarter final soccer cup game when one such storm began to roll in. It started to rain heavily and we could see thunder and lightning off in the distance but unfortunately it was heading our way. My team was winning by a goal to nil when the referee decided that, for safety reasons, the game should be postponed. Both teams left the field and we all huddled in a building corridor which led to the bathrooms. We had not been there more than a few minutes when there was an enormous clap of thunder which, by echoing off the corridor walls, almost blew out my ear drums. Within a split second a massive lightning bolt hit the field which made the hair on the back of my neck stand up on end. At this particular moment the storm was directly on top of us and if anyone had been on the rain soaked field they would have been killed outright. To say that we were all lucky is a vast understatement and the referee should be commended for his fore sight. This was the second time that I had defied the wrath of Thor, God of Thunder. The previous time was in Ann Arbor, Michigan and on that occasion three players were struck by lightning. While most of us ran to our cars, three players sought refuge under some trees that lined the opposite side of the field along the banks of the Huron River. They were all hit by a lightning bolt and unfortunately one of them died on the spot. I learned that day that it does not pay to roll the dice with Mother Nature because you just might cash in all of your chips. Death is forever and, as they say, forever is a long, lomg time.

Eleven
Unbroken Spirit

Iusually begin my day across the street from my house at the Gulf Drive Café where I have a cup of coffee with endless refills. This is almost a daily routine to try and get me brain in gear for the day to come. I usually sit outside, on the back porch, where the ocean can be scanned for dolphins, manatees and other delights of nature. If possible I sit at the end table, nearest to the open air deck, which affords me the opportunity of seeing all of the morning's visitors and activities. This has been my routine, early in the morning, for the past almost ten years and it has become such an obvious routine that people know where to find me if they need me. People who only visit our island once a year, for two or three weeks, walk in and shake my hand and catch up on current affairs. The waiters and waitresses there jokingly say that I should ask the owner to put me on the pay roll. Then instead of them having to field customer questions, they can just refer them to me. They should make my current unpaid advisory activities into becoming a permanent and official local meet and greet person. With my"gift of the gab"this should be a shoe-in for me and I could also direct their attention to my books which I religiously carry and shamelessly promote all the time. It would be a win/win situation for both the café and me.

The Long and Winding Road

I talk to people there from virtually all over America, plus a good deal from Europe, who make Anna Maria Island their number one vacation spot every year or as often as they can. As well as the month to month holiday people we have more recently accommodated a good number of long weekend visitors. Quite a few of these are here for wedding functions. Over the past three years this island has been promoted, by our Manatee County Tourist Board, as being the ideal location to be married right on the beach. The other Saturday evening my wife and I walk down the beach to the Moose Lodge, a distance of approximately one mile, and we passed four weddings strung out along the sands. All these out-of-towners are happy to be here and have brought money enough to spend for that purpose.

My wife and I, because we live directly behind the Queen's Gate Motel, are frequently invited to join some wedding parties there for drinks at the ensuing receptions. Better still is the fact that all evening foods, drinks and entertainment does not cost us one brass nickel. We have been invited to American, Russian, Latvian, Greek and numerous other weddings of various nationalities. We have enjoyed the company of many people from many ethnic backgrounds, who we will probably never ever meet again in our lifetime. Maybe it is because I am in a good place, at my time of life, or because I now see the good in most people but right now I could not be happier. I am not wealthy but I live comfortably and there should come a time, in every person's life, when contentment is to be considered more than just acceptable. I deserve this, in my humble opinion, because I have made the monumental decision to move here and this could have gone severely wrong. However, for once in my life I got it right. The path of a person's life can be fraught with uncertainties and so often we hear about the bad things in life that it is uplifting to occasionally hear a success story.

On the street where I now live there are just seven houses and a condominium complex called Summer Sands. Of the houses there are only three that are live in all the year around. Ours, my next door neighbor Mrs. Baldwin, originally from Appleton, Wisconsin and Big Jim who, as a younger man, was a champion arm wrestler and had a bit part in a 1985 Sylvester Stallone movie called Over the Top. Jim not only appeared in the film but he also trained the supporting actors the finer points of the sport of arm wrestling. I know his arm wrestling exploits are a proven fact because I have seen his many large and ornate trophies. With Sharon and I being authors, Claire Baldwin being an artist and Jim being a part actor we have an eccentric and eclectic bunch of characters in this small neighborhood. This makes just four people in a street that is about two hundred yards long and can only be accessed from 10th, 11th and 12th Street North, in Bradenton Beach. Because of this it is an oasis of serenity to live in, as there is not rarely any through traffic and is so quiet that you can almost hear a pin drop. The other three, one million dollar new homes, directly across the street from my property, although privately own are currently only being used as rental properties. All three of these owner have told me that their intension is to stay up north for the remainder of their working years until retirement rolls around. They will then move south to occupy their houses here and enjoy their golden years of retirement.

During the hot summer months only five or six of the condominiums are occupied permanently and so it is extremely peaceful in this green and luscious land. I am usually out working in my yard for part of almost every day and have plenty of time to chat to my neighbors if needed. My garden is full of ornaments, lawn furniture, hammocks and other hanging objects of art. Likewise my front porch and back patio is adorned with wicker furniture, potted plants and more ornaments which are permanently there, day and night, and yet I have never had one single item stolen. I usually am still in the old habit of locking my three doors at night but sometimes I forget, one or other of them, and yet again, no trouble at all. So not only do I live in comfort and good health, I also have the added advantage of being carefree. I absolutely believe, as I have said before, that moving to live here, almost thirteen years ago, has added at least five years to my life's expectancy. By owning a stand alone house I also do not have to contend with other people's rules and regulations. This would not be the case if I lived in a condominium complex or a gated community where the over bearing House Owners Association literally drive you around the bend with their ridiculous whims and edicts. On my property I can do anything I like so long as it is legal and not offensive.

A second, and equally as important, feature of my life here is that since I have taken up playing soccer again I have become somewhat of an island celebrity. I am still not too bad of a player but that is not the reason why people associate with me. It is because no-one here, or anywhere else if I may be so bold, has ever known a person of my age play the game with such vigor or commitment. Since the Soccer League has begun, up at Anna Maria Community Center, I have never missed a game no matter how ill I felt or how injured I have been. Since I started playing organized team sports, at the age of ten years old, I have only ever missed a scheduled game because of major injury. Sometimes I would have to go to the trainer or the physiotherapist to get my aching and wounded body back to where I would be able to play. What ever it took and no matter the pain, when the whistle was blown to commence the game, I was there ready to perform the best that I could.

I so desperately enjoyed the thrill of victory, or even the agony of defeat, that I was mentally disciplined so that my whole week revolved around preparing for my games. Whatever I had to endure, to be at the game, did not matter. I have, by far, the oldest team in the League and two other players, who play with me, have exactly the same ethic. Rico, who is a forty-two year old from Germany and Zoran, a fifty-three year old from Croatia have exactly the same mind set as me. Maybe it has something to do with the times and places where we were born and brought up. Howeve, whatever it is, we can be relied upon to be on the field of conflict when the referee starts the game. I guess that I am a bit of an oddity but, never-the-less, I enjoy the notoriety which is lavished upon me. Whether I am walking the beach, riding the island trolley, having a meal at a restaurant or a cocktail at a local bar, I am almost always signaled out for kudos and admiration. I enjoy this social acceptance and I relish the camaraderie because it makes me feel accepted by all social classes and ages of our island residents. There never seems to be a lack of things to ponder or items to discuss and for a social butterfly, like me, this is the nectar that fuels my ego. But then, I never was backwards in coming forward.

To make a point, the other day I was having coffee and reading the"Islander"when a man and his female companion sat at the next table to me. I was so near to them that I could not help but overhear them speaking to each other. It became immediately obvious to me that the guy was from the Liverpool area as he had an immediately recognizable Scouse accent. I struck up a conversation with him only to find out that he had been a proffessional soccer player back in England. His name is Ian Marshall and during his illustrious career he played for some of the best clubs in Britain during that time. He played for Everton, Ipswich, Blackpool and Leicester over a period of around twenty years or so. He is now the Managing Director of his own Soccer Academy back home and he said that he would love to be able to do the same thing in Florida. This would enable him to stay here for about three monthe of the year instead of the current two to three weeks which he currently enjoys. I just so happen to have some contacts with soccer clubs in the Bradenton and Sarasota area and so I put him in touch with them. Who knows, if these two parties hit it off, perhaps Ian will be able to realize his pipe dream and be able to visit Florida for longer spells in the future. I am living in one of the best places in America where so many famous and interesting people, from almost all over the world, come to live. They see Anna Maria Island and almost immediately fall in love with it and strive to devise a plan as to how they can possibly stay longer. They endeavor to become involved with some venture that will enable them to stay on a more permanent basis. This island is cute with a capitol"Q."

Twelve
Island Living

Sometimes I just have to pinch myself to be reassured that my brain is taking in all of what my eyes are seeing. The kids, who are brought up on this island, have an idyllic life that can be replicated only in such far off places such as the sun soaked shores of California, Hawaii, Brazil, Australia or South Africa. The ocean life style coaxes them into an open air mode of operation and they always seem to be inventing new ways to entertain themselves in or around the water. In this care free place it is nothing to get on the island trolley and find several people going fishing with their rods and bait buckets in hand. They can get off at virtually any stop along the route and will be just a few blocks from the ocean.

The other day, for instance, I caught the island trolley going north to put some of my books in at Ginny & Jane E's Emporium. When I boarded the trolley it was full of young tanned men toting their surf boards. There was an air of excitement as the surfer dudes chatted about their earlier exploits on the waves. I asked one of them where they were all going and he replied that they had parked all their vehicles down on the south end of the island at Coquina Beach. Since the wind was pushing the waves in a south easterly direction they would get off the trolley, at the north end of the island near the Rod & Reel Pier, and then ride the waves all the way to the bottom end of the isle, a distance of about eight miles. They would then repeat this sequence for as often as it took before they decided that they had enough enjoyment. In other words they were going to idle the whole day away without a care in the world. Never the less, consider what adventurous tales that they would have to tell and, as history has proven, surfer dudes just love to spin gnarly yarns.

I have seen similar amounts of ingenuity apportioned to the idle pursuit of skate boarding. I was on the beach some time ago when, as I sat in my beach chair, I was passed by another young man who for want of a better description was para-boarding on the hard sand. By this I mean that it was a cross between para-gliding and skate boarding. He was standing on his skate board while being propelled along by the wind driving the parachute and, being quite windy that day, he was flying along at a great rate of knots. Once again he was heading south down the beach, with the prevailing winds at his back, to Coquina where he would board the trolley to go north and do it all over again. The alternative to this is kite boarding which is virtually the same but this time it is performed on the water, ocean that is, instead of on the beach.

On yet another day I was standing at the side of the road idly chatting to someone or other when. out of virtually nowhere, came a young man with a small two stroke motor mower engine attached to his skate board. He had devised this mode of transport to get him to and from the Beach House restaurant where he was working as a waiter. His contraption only did around twenty miles per hour but it was sufficient enough to get him back and forth to work. Unlike the other two ingenious ruses this one was accompanied by a crash helmet and knee pads as hitting the concrete is much more unforgiving than hitting the sand or water.

Another newly devised past time, for the brave of heart, is that of paddle boarding. In this case a person stands upright on a surf board and uses a canoe paddle to propel himself along. I referred to this activity in the masculine gender because as of yet I have not seen this, or any of the other previous mentioned options, being participated in by any of the farer sex. Paddle boarding should only be attempted when the ocean is calm. Even so an island man went missing about two weeks ago and, although his board was found, he was not and is missing presumed dead. The board was found at Fort Desoto Park, on the north side of the Tampa Bay channel, as that is where the tide took it. No-one knows how his fate was decided as there are many and various ways to die when one chances the mood of, what would appear to be, a calm and placid ocean.

I have learned, during my considerable lifetime, that a person has to take the good with the bad and accept the rough with the smooth. I tell my next story with a slight amount of trepidation because it might put me in a bad light with some people but it did happen and since this is an expose of sorts I must, in all fairness, be candid. My wife and I work hard and play even harder and when the weekend rolls around we are ready to go and paint the town. Because of this we are known, at all the island watering holes, as people who can get a little boisterous at times. We have been accepted by all the proprietors, up and down the isle, as persons of interest because we spend a goodly sum of money and expect in return to be allowed to have a modicum of enjoyment.

I was in a bar on this particular night when I accidentally broke a beer mug. I had been censured previously, by the manager of this establishment, for banging the salt shakers on the table tops during the "Margaritaville" song made famous by Jimmy Buffet. Now this beer mug was not a thin flimsy thing, it was the type that had the thick glass rim around the bottom. The fact that it broke when I set it down on the table, in a normal manner, led me to believe that it was already cracked. The manager came rushing over and although I protested my innocence he asked me to leave the premises. This manager was a miserable looking older guy who had a gaunt appearance and dour expression. He was keenly aware that the owner of the bar lived way up near Green Bay, Wisconsin and so no-one could plead their case to him. I let a few weeks go by and then I went in to see if we could mend fences but it developed into an argument and he announced, to all and sundry, that I was banned for life. In everyone's opinion this was totally over the top. Since the whole crowd in the bar were witnessing the event I decided to fire him a broadside. I looked him sternly in his eyes and replied"Whose life, yours or mine ? Because I have every intension to out live you". The line in the sand was drawn and I did not cross the threshold of that bar for close to seven long years.

Well, a few weekends ago Sharon and I were at the Drift In bar when I spotted a guy who used to work at the afore mentioned watering hole. I asked him if the old geezer still worked at the infamous bar to which he told me that he did not. Further more he went on to tell me that the old decrepit Dickensian manager had recently been fired as"Certain things had gone missing". I turned to my wife and told her to finish her drink as we had a long awaited date with destiny. We marched across the street and entered Valhalla with our heads held high. The entertainer, who had been there the night that I was asked to leave seven years earlier, grinned from ear to ear as he saw us come through the door. When he finished the song he was singing he made a public announcement to the whole bar, staff and all, as to how we were unjustly banned and then welcomed us back with a rousing cheer. That one thorn, which had deeply stuck in my side for all those years, was finally removed. I had been completely vindicated and life had returned to the care free days of yester year. A long time ago a person, whom I despised, said that when I died he would dance on my grave. I, never being lost for a quick retort, replied"I hope you do because I am getting buried at sea".

I am sure that when I was a teenager back in Wales, and later as a young man up in the Liverpool area, I probably did get myself in some scrapes. There is nothing that a rugged yet lightly educated coal miner or steel worker likes least of all than a smart mouth young whipper snapper. With my quick wit I tended to put my mouth in gear while my brain was still in neutral and cause annoyance with some slower witted people. However, as I grew older I learned the meaning of tact and in my adult years I have only had three run ins with, who I describe as, the bad guys.

The previous story accurately depicted the most recent event, of this sort, however, I shall now relate to you the other two. The first occurred up in Dearborn, Michigan within the first year of me arriving in America. It happened in a show bar on Michigan Avenue on the west side of the city. I wandered in at the middle of the show and I was walking around trying to find somewhere to sit. When some guy shouted at me to sit down and I, not knowing who he was, told him in the words of Shakespeare, the Bard of Avon, to"bag it".Unfortunately for me the guy was the owner of the bar and even before I could realize what was going on I was dragged out into the foyer where three bouncers used me as a punch bag. Luckily, from my recent rugby playing days, I was as hard as a rock and wise in the ways of protecting myself and so they were not able to harm me too much. After that I was deposited unceremoniously out in the alley and I was not even given back my entrance fee. A few ex-Vietnam soldier friends of mine wanted to go there with baseball bats and extract some form of revenge but I told them to let it go. Point noted and experience well learned.

The only other time that I have had a major problem in a bar was here on this island a few years back. My wife and I were shooting a game of pool at the Sports Bar when a big, tough looking dude put up money on our table to play the next game.

The Long and Winding Road

Now my wife is good looking and since I had heard, through the grape vine, that this hombre had just been released from prison, I could see that at the least provocation there would be trouble coming our way. Somewhere in the middle of the game the guy told me to tell my woman [except he used the female dog word] that it was her shot. I took the cue from Sharon and laid it on the pool table and told him that we refused to play with him any further. He came completely unglued and went off his rocker. He proceeded to launch into a tirade of slurs and called me everything but a white man. I told him that he might as well be throwing snowballs at the moon because I did not understand a damn word that he was saying. This infuriated him even more and just about the time, when I expected the worse to happen, three other young men jumped up and hustled him out through the door giving him a couple of well aimed punches which were thrown in for good measure.

Apparently throughout the evening this parolee had addressed other women, with similar distain and profanities, and they saw this moment as their chance to set the record straight. I guess that there is justice in the world after all. My wife and I have not gone into that bar since because wherever there are pool tables there is an unusual amount of testosterone and chest thumping involved. Generally this eventually leads to a confrontation of some sort or other. If Sharon and I have the urge to play pool we now do so at the Moose Lodge where, it can be said, the egos are at a lower level and the atmosphere is sublime. Hence the saying "I'd rather have a bottle in front of me, than a frontal lobotomy." While on the subject of the Moose, it has just been announced that our lodge, at Bradenton Beach, has more members than any other chapter in the whole of the United States. Being right on the beach it is a most exceptional place to visit.

Incidentally, just to show that I am not a complete scoundral and that I can sometimes be a nice guy. The other day I met a young man, at the beach, who was a complete stranger to me and he commented that he admired my Hawian styled shirt. Being in a benevolent mood, I gave it to him right off my back. The guy was absolutely flabbergasted, with my out pouring of human kindness, as he had never before experienced such unabated generosity. My philanthropic outburst was, however, slightly diminished by the fact that I had a further thirty or forty similar shirts, hanging in my closet, and this one was soon to be relegated to the garbage bin.. Well, as they say, it is the thought that counts.

Sharon with granddaughter Brooke.

Cousin Tommy gets a twister.

Sharon with dad, Homer and mom, Pat.

Lyn, son Richard and his wife, Laura.

Thirteen
Minor Transgressions

Some things in life irk me somewhat. Those slight peccadilloes that are not so over whelming that they can alter ones life but enough to make you want to question the sanity of those people that feel it is acceptable to operate in a particular and peculiar manner. One of these is the occasions when I see people bring their dogs into a restaurant where other people gather to eat. To begin with it is unhygienic and contrary to most civil laws but, at the very least, it is rude to impose a mere whim on other diners who might not even like dogs. I mean, have you ever heard of a human taking food to a dog kennel for the sole purpose of dining there. If a person did this he/she would be considered to be a raving nut case. A family dog becomes more than just a pet when the owners feel that it has to be included in every aspect of their lives. A working dog is an asset to anyone but a lap dog is an extension of its owners perception of himself.

A restaurant owner, who I personally know, was fined $1000 when a Food & Beverage inspector made a surprised visit, as they often do, and found that a lady customer had sneaked in a lap dog and was feeding it under the table. The owner protested her innocents but it was to no avail and while all this was going on the errant customer and her cur slipped away unnoticed. On another occasion while sipping coffee, on the outside deck of a local café, I personally witnessed a young woman enter a café with a two year old child. As the woman was putting the child into a high chair a dog, belonging to a customer seated next to her, went for the child. The woman was hysterical and the child was inconsolable and they were forced to leave. The dog owner, in his infinite wisdom, protested that his dog had never done that before just as if this apology made everything alright. What does it matter, the fact is that their dog should not have been there in the first place but dog owners can never admit to this as it would make them appear stupid.

I also talked to a waitress who told me that she also was attacked by a dog as she approached a table to take a customers order. As it happened it was in the winter time and she was wearing jeans and so the damage to her ankle was minimal but why should any of these people have to be victimized by a complete stranger's wayward dog Some dog owners enter a restaurant actually carrying their forlorn puppies and this reminds me of the story that Cleopatra used to travel in the company of baboons for the sole purpose of making her look more attractive. I wonder what a dog owner's reaction would be if one day I sat at the next table to them with a parrot on my shoulder. As it squawked and defecated on my shoulder I could explain to the pampered dog lovers that I simply could not leave my parrot at home as he would become upset. I have recently heard that some television channel is going to bring out programs specifically for pet dogs to watch and I am beginning to think that there is no end to this lunacy. Another thing that has puzzled me, for sometime, is concerning whether or not the dog ever has a choice as to which eatery he will be taken to on any given day. Dog gone it, there I go again thinking that dogs are human.

Have you ever stopped to consider how in vogue it has become for the richer preppy types to dress down so as to give the appearance that they are, in fact, salt of the earth working class kind of people. I refer specifically to the now common practice of people wearing jeans, shorts, shirts and other garments which, from being bought brand new, have holes in them. They are also faded with roughly sewn frayed seams, patches and the likes with loose thread hanging from them. This type of clothing must appeal to those people who actually work at some sedate non-strenuous jobs, where they do nothing arduous all day. People such as attorneys, accountants, realtors, bankers and the likes, all want to give the outward appearance of having spent their working hours laboriously toiling outdoors in the boiling sun. These people even buy brand new baseball hats with the frayed and tattered visor as they must surely have been out laying down asphalt or gandy dancing on some railway tracks all day.

If I would have saved all my old clothes, which were falling apart when I threw them away, and brought them out to be resold today, I would now be living high on the hog.. They say that if you live long enough you will most likely see what was once fashion become fashionable again. If this this so I predict that there will come a time when we will all be gadding about in togas whilst munching on bunches of grapes and giving the thumbs down to some poor bastard down in the bowels of a Gladiator's arena. Forgive my over imaginative flight of fancy as I am sure that we will never return to becoming such a decadent society. Never-the-less, if the people who are currently demonstrating this downward divergence in fashion, continue along their current path, it will not be too difficult to foresee a resurgence of clothes similar to those worn during the American Great Depression of the 1930's. Maybe some of them might get the hankering to wear a bib and brace and go train hopping and live on farm camps like the hobos of that period. Anything is possible when people get seriously addicted to the urges of fashion. While I am on the subject of clothing, when did it become fashionable for young women to ware pajamas bottom out and about in broad daylight ? I would also like to address young men and request them to please hoist their pants up because, and I am sure that I speak for countless thousands, when I say that I am not interested in seeing the crack of their arse. The person who designed low-rise clothes for ladies should also be taken to the stocks for public punishment. The sight of flesh dripping over the waist line and a view of the Great Rift Valley is not appealing. These are just a few more mindless fashion expressions of a tasteless class of people.

My next little gem of oddities for you to mull over is the tattooed lady syndrome. I am not talking about the discrete tastefully placed tattoo, I am referring to the current custom of some women to have multiple tattoos put in places where they, themselves, cannot even see them. They put them across their backs, across their upper chest between their breasts and their neck, up and down their arms and legs and, of course, that chicest of all places, just at the top of their buttocks. Some of these tattoos are not depictions of recognizable objects but are quotations, mottos or logos that a viewing person would have difficulty in reading. A person would have to try and decipher the meaning of them, so as to somehow connect the script to its owner and try to guess how they are possibly linked. Some women look like walking bill boards while others just look like freaks who have so much time on their hands that they can spend hours idling time away while someone else injects them with ink.

The tattoos that cannot be read by their owners are commonly called"tramp stamps"and I must believe that they are done for only one of two purposes. The first is that some ladies, that would otherwise not be noticed, want other people to pick them out as persons of interest. This might just work as an initial reaction but, after the novelty has worn off, those women return to their normal level of mediocrity. The other reason, I suspect, is for some women to appear that they belong to some group or gang of people and are warning other people not to mess with them. Either way these tattoos are a cry in the wilderness brought on by the Hollywood film industry in its delusional attempt to portray some women as being equally as tough as men. Tattooing originated in far off savage places and was brought back to civilization by ancient travelers and mariners. They had meanings and told stories of where the seaman had traveled and the exotic types of people that they encountered on their odysseys. Then other male groups adopted tattooing as a falsification of their exploits which over many years have become accepted. Now we have an explosion with tattoo shops popping up on almost every street corner and women flocking to them in a vain attempt to make themselves more noticeable Tattooing can become an addiction to some people who keep adding and adding tats until their bodies have not even one bare spot left.

Thank goodness for stick-on tattoos so that a person can see what it would look like before being saddled with it for the rest of their lives. Then there is the occasion that a permanent name is added to ones body and some years down the road that person is no longer in vogue. Now it takes another trip to the tattoo parlor to have that tattoo removed or disguised so it cannot be recognized. It appears to me that, in all this frenzy of ink, the only one profiting from this is the tattoo artist and I only hope that those needles are clean ladies. I think back to when I was a young lad, growing up in Wales, the only way that I could see a tattooed lady was to pay money to visit the traveling circus as it passed through my town. I would pay to see her because, just like the bearded lady, she was a complete oddity and was considered to be a total freak of nature.

We have many beautiful birds on this island, both human and avian, but my last pet peeve concerns one of them. Being located on the coast we have quite a few restaurants that are directly situated on the beach. These are the favorite eating spots of the tourists who come down to this area through the winter and spring months. However, some of the visitors do not heed the"Do not feed the birds"signs which are posted at these locations. The sign, although a general warning, is specifically directed at one bird in particular, I refer to the ravenous seagulls who have become so brazen that it is considered to be nothing more than a flying rat. You might see just one gull and think that feeding it should not present a problem but from the second that one bird is fed thirty or forty others will arrive literally out of nowhere. In their frenzy, to get at food, they will literally swarm and physically attack people into submission to such an extent that they end up having to run for safety.

I have actually seen gulls swoop down onto food that have been left on plates right after customers have abandoned their table. I have actually seen a gull swoop down and take food right out of a child's hand and I have also seen a gull swoop and take food literally off a diner's fork while she was seated at a café table. While people are bathing in the ocean I have seen gulls go into their carrier bags and hampers to pull food out and steal it. They are aggressively smart and have learned that where there are humans there is inevitably food and people only have to drop their guard, for a moment, and the thieving gulls will swoop. I have even witnessed sea gulls land on top of pelican heads and take fish out of their mouths before they were able to swallow them. Therefore I must plead, to all who come here, to never intentionally feed the gulls. as this only encourages them to be boulder and even more aggressive than they already are. It was once said that in a dooms day scenario only cockroaches and rats would survive but, from my experiences, I would respectfully suggest that the marauding seagull should be added to that dubious list of pestulance.It is better to be fore warned, about the habits of these piratical birds, than end up with sea gull egg on your face.

Fourteen
Friendships

I have led a wonderful life that has been filled with good health, good money, a smattering of good friends and, to a lesser degree, some good luck. My good health and looks are genetically transposed and so I can take no credit in these areas. The good luck, that I have encountered was serendipity, when I was younger, but more like good judgment as I grew older. The good friends that I have made along life's ever changing path, however, have afforded me much pleasure and a blessing that continues to give.

Numerous people can count the good life long friends, that they have made, on one hand. However, in my case I have been fortunate enough to have met and retained so many good friends from varying times in my life. It is difficult to list all of them as they are located in many different countries around the world. Throughout my lifetime I have been blessed with some absolutely first class friends and when I analyze my time, on this planet, it becomes obvious that I am connected, to virtually all of them, because of our involvement in team sports. Whether it was rugby, soccer or athletics which brought us together with other competitors it afforded me the opportunity to have made some absolutely wonderful friends. Just like myself these characters have stepped outside of their comfort zone to find out what happens when tribal lines are crossed. They weren't just satisfied to hear about it or talk about it, they were prepared to experience it first hand.

From my early days, in Wales, such people as Mansell Jones, Peter Morrell, John Harris and Trevor Roberts spring to mind. From my time in England, the likes of Pete Metcalfe, Barry Roberts, Pete Lister and the recently deceased Alan Haig come to mind. From my soccer days up in Michigan characters like Bobby Harrison, Hugh Lindsay, Jimmy Canfield, Mark Belinda, Art Gasiewicz and the late Mostyn Conner are prominent in my mind. I keep in touch, by phone, with all of the previously mentioned people who are still alive. From time to time we will meet and share stories of our past exploits on and off the field of play. As a matter of fact, Jimmy Canfield phoned us yesterday, from Michigan, to see if we were alright down here on the island after Hurricane Isaac had just passed through our area. Good friends will do that.

Now that I am down in Florida and have taken up playing soccer again. I have once more met a whole slew of new close friends and it gives me a good deal of fun to be part of their company. Such people as Rico Biessert, Darrin Wash, Oliver Peteriet, Zoran Kolega, Tim Tedesco, Paul Hayward, Chris Yabarra and Damir Glavin, to name but a few, all share the love of sport which brings us together as a band of brothers. We all come from different backgrounds and even different countries but we are united by our common goal to exert and test ourselves for the love of sport. We all get that adrenalin rush when we are suited up to play in a competitive game and we never give any consideration to the thought of losing. If we are injured, during the fray, it is considered part and parcel of the thing that we choose to do and there is no finger pointing or recriminations. This is the sporting spirit that I have been brought up with, from the age of ten years old, and these are some of the like minded people that are closest to me in body, spirit and mind.

While I am on this subject of friendships I would be remiss if I did not mention my wife's New Boston red-neck family. Sharon and I just recently visited Michigan to celebrate the graduation of her nephew, who we hardly ever see because that branch of the family lives in Midlothian, Virginia. The night before the family gathering I was asked by my brother-in-law, Danny, if I would like to accompany him to pick up the pig that was to be roasted at the next day's celebration. He told me that we had to go over to cousin Tommy's house and I naturally thought that the pig was there. Oh no ! Danny, Tommy, Tommy son T J and I all piled into a truck and took off down the road. After about thirty minutes I casually asked where it was that we had to pick up the doomed swine, to which I was told"Dundee". Although it was not Dundee, Scotland we still had quite a way to go, which included having to drive through a quaint little town called Maybe. If anyone asks if you have ever been there you can sincerely answer"maybe". Well we arrived at the farm in Dundee, after a one hour drive and then, as is the apparent custom, we all sat around with the farmer and his wife and had several toddies for the body. After a serious round table discussion concerning tractors, farm dogs, and crops, Tommy paid the farmer his money to cement the deal. The farmer then took us to the freezer room where the forlorn pig was hanging from a hook all nicely trimmed and ready for cooking. The pig left life weighing two hundred pounds but its trimmed weight was now around one hundred and twenty and this was considered enough to feed sixty to eighty party goers.

While drinking some beers, as I sat in the back seat of the truck on the way back, it occurred to me that without a doubt I had definitely married into a red-neck family. These good old boys see life in a different light than other folks and, if times become real hard, I would rather be in their corner. They have learned how to scrape by when times are tough and they also have a network of other good old boys to help them along the way. City people might be book smarter but when it comes down to the nitty gritty of it all, I will take my chances with my country cousins. I am proud that they have kindly accepted me into their lives, their homes and their families. I have learned to appreciate them more than words can tell.

Again while on the this subject, in August of this year, my wife and I are off to Ireland for a wedding there. My good pal Pete Metcalfe, from my Port Sunlight Rugby Club days, is marrying off his youngest son Matt to a beautiful young Irish lassie named Edel. The event is in the northern part, of that divided land, in the county of Tyrone. The wedding is in the girls home town of Sion Mills and the reception is at a hotel on the outskirts of city of Derry called, would you believe, The Everglades.. I left England in 1976 and for two years, prior to that, I visited Northern Ireland every month. I had a business office in the town of Lisburn just south of the capital Belfast. Around that time the situation there was troublesome and the atmosphere was bleak and frightful and so it will be my great pleasure to see this land in a new light and in better times.

Both Matt and his elder brother Adam was in the next generation of players at Port Sunlight R.F.C. after Pete and I. From some of the stories that I have heard, they did the club and their family name proud. Their mother Maureen, or Mo as she is lovingly referred to, religiously took those two boys up to watch the games that their Dad and I played in. I wish that I could say that we taught them all that they know about the game but the boys were just toddlers in those days. I clearly remember being told, by the great Port Sunlight bard Aghi, of the game where Port Sunlight won a junior cup final at Birkenhead Park and out of the fifteen players that day three Metcalfe men were in the team --- Pete, Adam and Matt. Now there's one for the record book and something that I suspect will never be replicated again, at least not in my lifetime.

The Long and Winding Road

When I played soccer up in Michigan, here in the USA, I played along side two brothers from the City of Derry, named Charlie and Gary Bell. At that time they were probably halve of my age but never the less it was nice to play along side them. Charlie settled down in the States and now has a wife and a couple of children while Gary is now back in the old country. I made a guest appearance for the Canton Celtics, a few years ago, when they came down here to Florida. That day Gary Bell drew the goal keeper out of his net and put me through for an easy goal which won us that game. This is even more amazing when I say that Gary took me aside, directly before that goal and told me exactly what he planned to do and quite honestly, he made me look like a hero. Gary slept in my garage for a couple of nights and then took off back to Michigan and I have never clapped eyes on him since. Sometime later I heard that he dropped out of college and since he was in America on a student visa, he was picked up by the Immigration authorities and deported back to his homeland.

Since I am going to be virtually in Gary's back yard I am going to see if I can locate him after all these years. With me dropping in to his home town, out of the blue, what a shock it will be for him and I can't wait to see the look on his face. The last time that we parted company he needed a warm coat, for his journey back up north, and so I gave him one of mine. If the weather is bad, while I'm over there, perhaps I can borrow it back. Also, I was watching a game of Gaelic Football on the television, here in the States, and one of the teams was from County Down. As it showed that county's team sheet before the game started, there were an abnormally large percentage of players with"Clarke"as their last name. They were all from a town in County Down [I'm a poet and didn't know it !] and the idea struck me that if I ever found myself in Down, I would look up the town which they all appeared to come from. I have never heard of it before but it is called Ballygilget. It must be quite a small town because

I have looked it up on an Irish atlas map and it does not show up at all. It could be one of those towns, over there, where the local post office doubles up as an ale house and you can probably have your hair cut there as well. It will be great if all the Clarke clan can meet for a party, or ceileh as they call it, and have one massive wing ding of a get together with some Guinness and Irish music thrown in for good measure. This would be another item that I can cross off my bucket list.

Fifteen
Fire Down Below

I was born at a period in history when my family had seen better times. We were not considered to be poor but with my father's death, during World War II, our families financial situation instantly changed for the worse. In fact it was much more severe than that because this shattering event also turned our family's world upside down. Because of all this I suffered the slings and arrows of discontent and this made me resolve, at an early age, that one day I would be rich. I had no set plan or any idea how this would come about but I had fire in my belly. This made me ever vigilant for any money making opportunity, no matter how small, that I could grasp to make my life better.

At first these random opportunities, for making extra money, were small and quite insignificant but as I became a little older and a little wiser my ideas to make extra money, became bigger and more daring. For instance, in my early days a person would pay me a small amount of money to track down some information about a source where he could find a particular product or service. After a while it dawned on me that instead of giving him this information, to act on,I could make money from both ends if I played the role of broker. In other words by being the middle man I could make money from the supplier if

I bought his product or service and I could then make money, from the end user, by reselling it to him at a marked up price. No longer was I going to sell myself short by giving away my sources of information. Because of this stroke of genius I set myself up as a general factotum and became extremely adapt at searching out supplies of scarce items for people who did not have the time, or know how, to do so themselves. It became abundantly clear to me that knowledge was a premium and it was this factor that was the difference between the"haves"and"have not."

One such instance occurred when I was working in Michigan and concerned a manufacturer of a special type of tooling. One mile up the road, in the same town, was another company that was buying the same tools from a foreign company and complained to me about their long deliveries. I put the two companies, who were previously ignorant of each other's existence, together and received a finders fee from the one firm and commissions from the supplier on every order,on this deal, ad infinitum. I made deals like this over and above my full time employment pay and being a salesman, as I was from aged twenty four onwards, I had all the freedom in the world to seek out and act on any such opportunities that came my way. Do I feel a sliver of guilt because of my double dealing ? Absolutely not because I had already discovered how disloyal companies can become when it suits them. My decision at an early age, never to be poor again, was my inspiration and driving force and as I moved into this mode of operation I didn't even give the integrity of it a second thought. I was the alley cat who stole the rich man's cream and licked my lips with satisfaction. It was a case of where there's a will, I want to be in it. This extra money made the difference between living comfortably or living high on the hog. There was not a shadow of a doubt, in my mind, that I would never feel the humiliation of being poor ever again while I had a single breath left in my body.

Consequently, as my life progressed I always had a second source of income which would give me more monies so that I could afford to do those extra little things that made life so much more enjoyable. Outside of my main jobs I have independently owned and operated around a dozen or so side jobs and businesses. These gave me the standard of living that I craved for as a boy growing up in Wales. I have been a manufacturers representative with several product lines. I had my own household cleaning products company. I have owned and operated my own retail sporting goods stores and my own public telephone company. I have worked for a city's recreation department and separately I have coached soccer teams. I have designed and printed tee shirts to resell for various teams, functions and organizations and I have bought and sold flags and banners for various international social clubs. On weekends I ran a booth selling sports clothing and footwear at an open air market and I have even tried my hand at painting and decorating. When money is short no task can be considered beneath you.

As you can see I did not stay in any one sector of business but went into any sphere of opportunity where I could see a chance to make extra money. I have even repaired and paved parking lots and drive ways with asphalt just because a customer told me that he was having trouble finding someone to do it for him. This all seems rather slap dash but it taught me that I could turn my hand to almost anything, outside of brain surgery, if I put my mind to it. Once that barrier was removed, from my mind, there were so many new profitable endeavors to consider where extra monies could easily be made. This can be achieved if a person can open up his mind and strip away the old fashion veneer of only having one job description. This has been drummed into us, all our lives, and has deprived us all from an abundance of new opportunities which could possibly have made our lives so much more fruitful.

Lyn Clarke

I am now retired and have started a new part-time career of book writing and, along with my wife, we have also produced and published seven books of our own. Then other people began to tell us that they also have always had the desire to write their own book and have it published. Well, if you now understand how my brain operates it will not take you too much time to work out that I am now publishing books for other people. Having learned the hard way, and lost a considerable amount of money in the proceedings, experience has taught me all the pitfalls that inexperienced authors can get into. With my first book I paid an agent $2,000 to help in having it published and have come to find out that if a writer is not famous or a person of note, no amount of money in the world will induce anyone to publish your manuscript. This exercise was completely futile and for me it wasted the better part of two years.

I almost signed up with a publishing house where I would be expected to sign away all rights to my work and who charged so much for me to buy the finished book that it would have been almost impossible to resell them. Eventually I found a small publishing house that produced my first book but it still cost me the best part of $2,200 I transferred my second book to yet another house which was cheaper but still a little too costly. After around four years had passed by I had the brilliant idea of self publishing and now the cost is attractive enough for me to get a good product, at a reasonable cost, for the authors to be able to sell their books at an attractive price and everyone is happy. All of these trials and tribulations have made me a more efficient business person and, let's face it, the only way to learn is by making mistakes which invariably will cost money. This is what is called paying your dues and the acid test is to never make the same mistakes twice. Thus the adage that all is well that ends well.

I have basically always been an optimist but as one ages this has to be tempered with a certain amount of caution. Now if you consider that you can do this, by balancing these two attributes, then very likely you are a gambler. I don't necessarily mean that you spend umpteen hours a week sitting at the black jack table or feeding tokens into a one armed bandit at your nearest casino. What I mean is that you probably like to bet on an occasional game, team or sporting event. I also enjoy the occasional flutter on the horses or dogs and infrequently play the slot machines but never for any large sums of money. Some time ago I convinced myself that I had cracked the code for winning the six number lottery game that is played up in Michigan twice per week. I will not divulge my secret formula but suffice to say that having played my system twice a week for around eighteen months I finally succeeded to select all six numbers. I double checked the numbers, listed in the local paper, and there was no doubt that I had selected all of the six numbers for that drawing. On that day I had bought two lines of numbers and so it now remained for me to see where my numbers fell. Would you believe I had the last three numbers in the first line and the first three numbers in the second line which afforded me the payment of exactly zero dollars.

The odds against anyone picking all six numbers are several millions to one and for me to surmount those odds and come out of it with nothing is tantamount to treason. If just one of those numbers had been in the other line I would have at least been paid $100, but not a penny. Just when someone thinks that they know all the answers, life has a way of drop kicking that person right in the groin to affect an immediate attitude adjustment. I now consider it silly of me to dare to try and outwit Lady Luck because many have tried and many have failed. From here on I will keep my optimism at a reasonably controlled level so as not to be tempted to be overly confident and, therefore, avoid having my ego shattered into little pieces.

Earlier, in this book, I listed a team of rugby players from back in Pontypool's hay days. One of those names was of a man whose name was Paynter. Each time that I type this name my computer's spell check will warn me that this is miss spelled and so it has lodged in my mind. Last Saturday was the 2012 Belmont Stakes, the third leg of the illustrious Triple Crown and a horse called Paynter was entered. Well, this was too much of a coincidence for me to pass up and so I picked it to win. This horse led from the starting gate to a stride from the winning tape where it was beaten by a neck. This is just another example of how Lady Luck leads me on and then dashes my hopes and dreams at her whim. What a fickle mistress she has turned out to be.

I would like to make it absolutely clear that in my latest and possible last endeavor, that of book publishing, was not entered into as a capital venture. My publishing company was developed because I could see that there were many other budding writers who needed assistance in bringing their works to the public and, by definition, this is what publishing is all about. I hope to resolve, for unknown writers, the issues of finding a publisher and to help solve for them all the complications of this process. I am hoping to be a voice for all those brilliant, yet undiscovered, authors by getting their books to the market place Being a writer myself I know just how important it is to help these people who have the same passion about writing books, as I do, and to help them to get their message out for the reading public. I feel good about what I am doing and I see myself somewhat as a present day Robin Hood, taking from the rich and redistributing to the poor. Yes, I will make some money but what I am offering, to other budding authors, is the least expensive method of having their dreams fulfilled. The small amounts of money, that I will make will only slightly offset the large amounts which I have already lost while traveling down the stony path of the major publishing industry of the current times.

I have recently heard of another lady who is attempting to do the same thing and a thought has flashed through my mind that perhaps one day there could be enough of these small publishing companies, that some kind of association might be formed to give this cause an even greater presence. However, for the time being, I am content to assist authors, one at a time, with their hitherto unheralded endeavors. Writing and publishing should not be a pleasure for just the rich and famous and this has been resoundingly proved by the success of J. K. Rowling, an unknown author who is now famous around the world. She began writing stories to amuse her young son because she could not afford to buy books for him. Now that's a great story.

Sixteen
The Sporting Mecca

I have just completed my perpetual morning ritual of having coffee across the street at the Gulf Drive Café. I meet the most interesting people who come there from virtually all over the world. Sometimes, through the buzz of activity, several different foreign languages can be heard and this gives the café an international flavor. It is somewhat comforting for me to think that people wake up, in their native lands, and excitedly get on a plane so that they can come to this amazing destination. This location has become a magnet for the knowledgeable world wide travelers and it is awesome to think that where I have chosen to live out the rest of my life, has become a tourist hotspot

About five miles from where I am currently residing is the International Media Group [I.M.G.] Academy which, in the sporting world has become to sports afficinadoes what Mecca is to Islamic pilgrims. Budding stars in the tennis, soccer and golfing spheres of sport are lined up for the chance of being invited here to further their sporting dreams and careers. This morning three bright eyed young men came into the cafe and sat at the next table to me and their demeanor told me that they were athletes. They were each in the sixteen to eighteen age range and, as a young man can, they ordered and ate enough food to feed a battalion.

After a furious five minutes, of avidly bolting down their breakfasts, they settled back in a more relaxed posture. It was at this point that I struck up a conversation with them and found out which sporting endeavor had brought them to my doorstep.

It turned out that they happened to be soccer players one each coming from Switzerland, Nicaragua and Porto Rico. I spoke with the more talkative of the three, who was aptly nicknamed Gabby, and being inquisitive I asked him if they were in the category of pupil who paid their way or whether they had been invited to come on a scholarship. He told me that they had originally come to I. M. G. for a paid clinic but had each been singled out, as being talented, and were invited back on an all expense paid scholarship. Now this puts these young men in a distinct category of athletes that have a very good chance at becoming rich and famous in their field of sport. Just like the continual stream of tennis players, who have been trained at that location, these three young men are on course to be some of the best up and comers in their sphere of sport. I firmly expect to hear that these young players have made a name for themselves, somewhere down the line.

My pal Jeff, one of the waiters at the café, told me that he had met a young man from England who was also bound for the same academy of excellence here in Florida. Jeff was returning from a trip to England where he had visited his wife and new baby down in the Celtic shire of Cornwall. The young soccer player was on his flight out of London to Charlotte, North Carolina and again on the leg of the journey from Charlotte down to Tampa, Florida. This will give some idea concerning the scope of I. M. G. and the lengths that they go through to ensure that they find the absolute best young starlet in each of the sports that they are involved with. The intense training and the mental fortitude that these boys, and girls, are put through will almost certainly put them on track for an extraordinary future. After a nice chat the boys began to leave but even before they had stepped away from their table, people were asking for a photo to be taken with them. So, for them, notoriety had already arrived and soon the money will naturally follow.

I have avidly watched the Wimbledon Tennis Tournament over the years and when unknown players arrive, out of the blue and does extremely well, you can bet your bottom dollar they have been trained right here by the famous sports motivator Nick Bollettieri. Maria Sharapova lives near here and trains at this famous academy and if these young men can earn half of the money that she has, over the years, they should be very happy and contented. Maria, incidentally, has just become one of an elite group of women tennis players by winning the 2012 French Open Tournament. She can now add this trophy to the English [or Wimbledon] Australian and USA titles which she won before a shoulder operation side lined her for around three years. I still regret the fact that I have played sport, at a more than reasonable level, for fifty odd years and never was paid a plugged nickel. That makes me about as happy as a turd rolled in cracker crumbs.

Where there is joy unfortunately there is invariably tragedy lurking in the back ground eagerly awaiting to appear. At the same café, just a few months ago, the serene morning was disturbed by a shattering event. As usual I was deeply engrossed in my daily crossword and Sudoku puzzles when I heard one of the waitresses say that someone had just been knocked down by a vehicle directly in front of the building. There is a pedestrian walkway to and from the café and this person, a lady in her late sixties, had stepped into the cross walk and was hit by a passing van. The lady driver of the van, who was around the same age as the victim, had taken her eyes off the road,for a moment, to glance at the beautiful ocean. A few seconds is all that it took for the two to meet and in these types of collision the vehicle always wins. From where the lady was struck to where she landed was around thirty yards in distance.

About five minutes prior to this occurring an elderly couple came in and sat at the next table to me and I heard them tell their waiter that they would place their food order when their sister arrived. When I had become aware of what had happened outside I appraised them of the event which had just occurred and, sure enough, when they went outside to check on the situation, tragically it was their sister lying on the road. Pandemonium ensued as police cars, fire trucks and ambulances converged at the accident scene and the lady was rushed of to the nearest hospital. Unfortunately, with the severe wounds which she had sustained, she passed away at the hospital a short time later. Her relatives, who had innocently set out that morning to rendezvous with her for breakfast, were devastated. Even in the Garden of Eden there was a serpent and thus no matter how wonderful the surrounds are, you should never let your guard down, not for even a second.

I have heard recently that the police are not pursuing charges against the woman driver because they have come to the conclusion that she and the pedestrian were equally to blame. Incidentally, down here in Florida, and possible some other States with which I am not familiar, have the annoying habit of leaving a deceased body lie where it ends up until a certified Medical Officer can turn up and decree that the person is actually dead. Forgive me if my judgment is awry but if the body has not stirred, for an hour or so,would it not be prudent for someone to check a pulse to ensure that the unfortunate person is, in fact, still with us or not. To see a body stretched out on the floor, while being covered with a white sheet, is not the best way for anyone to begin their day. Even the most primitive people, from the most uncivilized regions of the world, know that this is not the way to act in these dire circumstances. A little more dignity needs to be injected into the proceedings.

While I am on a down note and with a more trivial matter, I must report that my soccer season has just ended as my team was unceremoniously bounced out of the play offs at the quarter final stage. It was an extremely difficult season for my team because we were, by far, the oldest team in the league. On a full sized field with a goal keeper and just six others players, we had a tough time trying to keep up and handle the younger set. Out of the nine games that we played we won three in good style, narrowly lost four even though we put up a commendable struggle and lost two further games where, for one reason or another, we could not get our game together and did not play at all well. The last of these games was a five goals to one loss to the same team that we had narrowly lost to, with a score of six goals to five, just a few games earlier. In that game with five minutes to go, we were winning five goals to three but as our old legs ran out of steam and we were pipped at the post. Incidentally, the team that beat us, that day, went on to win the tournament final which gave us some form of satisfaction and made them worthy and indisputable island champions.

I originally had eleven players on my roster but two of my younger players were injured and had to drop out for reasons beyond their control. This left me with nine players on my squad for the play off game and on the night of the game my two best players turn up injured. Zoran is a tennis coach at I. M. G. and had twisted his knee during a practice session the previous day. My other star player, Rico, had played all season with pain in both his knees and, during this game, he could barely hobble around the field. Mark, a good utility player was troubled with back spasms and on top of all this Missy, my best female player phoned me, that very afternoon, to say that she had decided to permanently move back to New York State. I asked her if she could make that night's vital game but she was already in Georgia on her journey home. I knew before the kick-off that with my team in this shape it was going to be an inevitable disaster. From the start, with our younger opponents running all over us, there was only going to be one result. As gallant as we were the final outcome was never in doubt and we now have all the time in the world to rest up and lick our wounds.

For me, at the age of seventy-two, it is the end of what was once a glittering career. I can no longer compete with the eighteen year olds that are now allowed into the league and who are a quarter of my age. I will contain my sporting activities with my twice a week kick about games and leave the serious competitions to my younger counterparts. As a wise man once said"All good things must come to an end"and it is with deep regret that I have come to this decision. I have always preferred to die with my boots on but not necessarily with my soccer boots on. It has been one heck of a ride, filled mostly with excitement and a little anguish but there are endless memories of good times and good people that will fill my heart and mind until, inevitably, the lights go out.

Hold the press, since writing my soccer obituary, which pronounced my impending retirement, right out of the blue I was selected as a last minute replacement to play in the end of season All Star game. I played for Team Black and, in a spirited exhibition game we emerged as winners by three goals to two over Team White. Our team consisted of Chris [Turkey], Zoran and Damir [Croatia], Scott, Josh, Rio and Leslie {USA] and myself {Wales]. I played at left full back and performed well which always makes the game enjoyable.

After the game, because of my impending retirement, I was bombarded with well wishers and most of them expressed the view that they hoped to see me again as I obviously still had the ability and the will to play. It is quite amazing how one good game can give a person the lift needed to inspire one to continue. Because of this unscheduled event, I will ponder on this situation throughout the summer months. Who knows, I might decide to dust off my boots and take another run at it when the fall season comes around I would, without a doubt, miss all the comradeship and the obligatory after match morale boosting parties where the alcohol takes over and transforms mere mortals into gods After many years of playing competitive sports, I have learned that players only love you when your playing.

The next sporting activity is one that I never thought, for a moment, that I would come in contact with. In the passed few years I have reacquainted with a guy that I used to run the bars with up in Michigan back in the late 1970's. His family has owned and operated a famous burger bar in the Detroit area for the best part of seventy years. He has two sporting passions the one being golf, which is quite normal, but the other is going on safaris to Africa to participate in big game hunting. This Earnest Hemingway styled sport is rare, significantly expensive and not for the faint of heart. I do not entirely agree with the killing of wildlife, however, the manner in which this is carried out, in an African wild life preserves, they only allow selective animals to be culled. There is also a rigid quota system which is imposed to ensure that only a limited allotted number of animals may be taken. This is strictly monitored by game wardens who usually accompany the hunters on safari. The wildlife is not artificially lured, with food, into a killing zone and ambushed and so all kills is done by tracking and shooting on the fly. These animals are not shot from a camouflaged hunter's hide which,incidentally, I find unfair and distasteful.

The people who run these wildlife refuges are seasoned professionals and do not allow any random or unauthorized killings to take place. On my recent trip, to the Detroit area, my long lost pal invited me to his house to view his big game hunting trophies and they were, to say the least, extremely impressive. I mention this only because during all my years of travel and all the people that I have met along the way, this is the only occasion where I have encountered a real life big game hunter. My pal always was unusually brave as was proved when he stepped on a land mine during in the war in Vietnam, and spent a whole year recuperating from his back injury. Perhaps all the shooting he did, during that conflict, has made him the marksman that he is today.

Cap'n Stretch, the white Heron pays a visit.

The three magic wells at Gunverston.

Sunset at Bradenton Beach.

Celtic burial sight at Lanyan Coit.

Seventeen
Airport Howlers

As you can well imagine I have traveled quite extensively in my vicarious life and a good percentage of this has been by aero-plane. I have flown on jumbo jets, I have flown on business class jets, I have flown on ten seated biplanes and I have flown on two seated crop sprayers. The only type of flying machine that I have not, nor ever will fly on, is an ultra light like the one that John Denver, one of my all time favorite singers, crashed and died in. I have had some hair raising occurrences and I have had some head scratching experiences mainly brought on by my own lack of fore sight.

Take, for instance, the occasion when my wife Sharon and I were flying out of Tampa airport to England. We had already gone through the metal detector check point and we were sitting down at the departure gate. Sharon went to retrieve an item, from a piece of hand luggage, when she realized that we didn't have the bag. After the ex-ray check we had put our shoes back on and collected all our small pocket items and scurried away leaving a small carrier bag behind. We had to dash back to retrieve it and, of course, we were met by a band of armed security guards with grim faces. Although this incident was a small oversight, on our part, the security guards took the whole incident extremely seriously and they were by no means amused.

Then there was the time when, once again, we were flying out of Sarasota Airport, and approached that daunting ex-ray check point. We took our shoes off and emptied all metal objects from our pockets and as I approached a security guard I patted my shirt breast pocket to ensure that I had not forgotten anything. The guard, a little Hispanic lady, requested that I step out of line and wait, which I thought was somewhat odd. After about ten minutes of watching endless people going through the check point and Sharon by now waiting for me on the other side, I asked the guard why it was that I had to wait. She replied that, because of my heart condition, I would have to wait for special clearance at which point I replied that I didn't have a heart condition. She said that she saw me patting my heart, which is an international signal to indicate that I had a bad heart. I explained to her that what she observed was me patting the pocket, located over my heart, to ensure that it was empty. Well that was ten minutes of my life that I would like to get back and so, readers beware, do not make any unnecessary movements, at this juncture, in case they might be misinterpreted.

Yet another howler happened when Sharon and I were flying out of Detroit Metro airport back to Florida. We had a 7:00 AM flight and so we were up two hours earlier so that we could grab a quick bite to eat and have a lift to the airport. We arrived at our gate, for the Detroit to Atlanta leg of our journey, and to our surprise, there was no-one on duty to check us in. We waited for about another twenty minutes, and still the gate had not been opened and I said to Sharon that I felt that something was amiss. I rechecked our tickets only to realize that we were completely at the wrong gate. The gate number that we were at was the number for our second flight, from Atlanta to Tampa, and I had looked at the wrong ticket. If you can imagine the shape of a banana, we were located at the one end of that shape and, would you believe it, the gate that we were supposed to be at was situated at the very opposite end of that shape. We rushed as fast as we could, with all our luggage, but when we finally arrived at the correct gate the flight had boarded and, although it was still at the gate, we were refuse entrance. Luckily for us there was another flight, from a near by gate, one hour later and we were able to get on and we still made our connecting flight at Atlanta. You can put this one absolutely down to me as not being completely awake at that ungodly hour of the morning. Those red eye early morning flights are just killers and tend to reduce me to being a man of constant sorrow.

To further illustrate my continued ineptness, brought on by old age, I invited a woman friend from Wales, who had recently lost her husband after several years of illness, to come to Florida to stay with us. After rethinking the distance involved and with her traveling alone I told her, that if she wanted to, she could bring along a companion and so she invited her niece to travel with her. My wife and I drove up to Tampa airport and the arrangement was for them to deplane, collect their luggage and we would be waiting, with the car, parked right outside at the arrival doors. The outside flight board indicated that their plane had landed and so I told Sharon that I would go inside and wait, at the foot of the escalator, which they would have to descend to retrieve their luggage. Some passengers from that flight began to trickle down and one of them told me that most of the passengers were waiting, up on the top deck, to be collected.

This having been told, I went up and sure enough there they were. We then came down to the lower level and picked up their luggage and went outside but Sharon and the car, by this time was not there. I should explain, at this juncture, that drivers are not allowed to stay parked at the curb side indefinitely. Because of this I assumed that she had been asked to move on and was in the process of making a lap of the airport before returning to pick us up. We stood there, with the luggage, for around forty five minutes and still no Sharon. At this juncture I knew something was amiss and on glancing up, to check our location, I realized that we were at the complete opposite side of the terminal arrival building from where we should be. We beat a hasty retreat to the other side and, sure enough, there was the now frustrated Sharon parked at the curbside. We bundled into the car with all the luggage and for some inexplicable reason I could not stop laughing about the complete absurdity of the whole situation. However, this did not go down too well with the, by now, extremely frustrated Sharon. We can all laugh about it in retrospect but how I came down the escalator, on the wrong side of the building, is a fact that I still cannot explain. I guess it was just one of those senior moments that creeps up on a person of my age and the less said about it the better.

The funny thing about that whole fiasco is that the very same thing happened to my son Richard, at the very same airport, when he flew in to visit us a few years earlier. He came down the wrong escalator and was waiting, in the wrong place, for me to pick him up while I was sitting in my car on the opposite side of the building. He traveled with just a carry on bag and when he deplaned he went directly down the wrong escalator and outside to the curb. After not finding me for around thirty minutes he phoned Sharon, at our home, then she in turn rang me to tell me where he was waiting. Then I drove the car around to the other side of the arrivals building and picked him up from where he had been standing all the time. It seems that the older one gets the more complicated life becomes and it is not the major things in life, that become troublesome and difficult, it is the minor stuff that seems to throw a wrench into the works. Small things like replacing the zipper on ones pants before exiting the toilet is worrisome. However, even this pales into insignificants when compared with forgetting to release ones zipper before urinating. Which proves that I'd rather be pissed off than pissed on.

For your information [FYI] on a very recent flight, from Tampa to Detroit with Delta Airlines, we dutifully checked in our rolling suit cases in the expected manor. This kind and thoughtful act, on our part, was to alleviated the over loading of a capacity filled flight and for this privilege we paid $25 per case, over and above our air fares. When we assembled at the departure gate, prior to take off, we noticed that there was a slew of passengers who still had their rolling suit cases with them. Then half way into the boarding procedure the gate attendant made the announcement that because the flight was so full and all storage spaces were already taken, anyone with rolling suit cases would be allowed to stow them in the plane's hold for free. Well you could have knocked me over with a feather and I guess the moral of this little anecdote is to do unto others before they do unto you. On the return journey, being now somewhat wiser, we did not check in our rolling suit cases and, as previously, they were stowed in the plane's hold for free. If you screw me once, shame on you but if you screw me twice, shame on me.

I have traveled extensively during my lifetime, some for pleasure but mostly for business. I began my career as a salesman in 1964 and took an early retirement in 2002 and during those years I traveled throughout Britain, Scandinavia, Western Europe and three quarters of the United States of America. I have probably flown over a million miles and right now I only fly for pleasure. I figure that if a plane, that I am traveling on, is destined to go down then it will have been my choice to be on it and not the case that I am flying on a business trip for the benefit of someone else. Since the infamous 09/11 terrorist incident, flying has become more of a chore than a pleasure and so I now consider hard and long before taking a flight for any reason or to any destination.

Traveling by plane became so second nature to me that I could walk into any airport bar and pick out, just by observation, who was on vacation and who was on business. The holiday makers were always upbeat and full of anticipation while the business travelers were more subdued and serious in their appearance. This was especially true at the end of the week when the business flyers were returning home after a grueling week of meetings and negotiations. These characters would be staring blankly into their drink of choice and only altered their focus if a pretty young lady, traveling alone, came in and sat near to them. Then being the salesmen that they are, their demeanor would instantly change and they would endeavor to engage the occasional traveler with conversation.

The only other signs of activity, from these business types, is if they find another salesman, in a similar line of business, when they could regale each other with their fetes of salesmanship. These sessions were particularly productive when the salesmen compared notes and swapped vital contact names. The sales game is a dog eat dog business where only the fittest and sharpest survive and it is true that a company only rates a salesman by his previous month's sales achievements. The Chairman of a company that I once worked for refused to accept a $50,000 order, which I had brought in, on the grounds that it did not fit his perceived future production plans. Two months later the same Chairman laid me off because, in his words, incoming orders were down and so the company's business was in a slump. How ridiculous was that and what a sad comment on a once noble profession.

Eighteen
Nothing Stays The Same

Although one would not immediately notice, without study-ing the situation at length, what in the main appears to be the same invariable changes. The changes may be muted and subtle to the naked eye but never the less changes they are. My soccer pal P. J. Smargisso and his family have taken over the Banana Cabana Grill and Restaurant and serve up some of the very best Caribbean cuisine that money can buy. Order P. J's mango glazed stuffed island grouper or Mike's Caribbean curry, as they will make your mouth water with anticipation. For dessert try one of my favorites which are the Key Lime pie or the fried banana macadamia both of which I heartily recommend. The food is always accompanied with live music provided by some of the best local entertainers on the island. So get in there early and bring a big appetite because you are in for a treat.

Bertie [Roberta] and her husband Jeff Levey, from Ginnie and Jane's Emporium, have recently taken over the Martiniville Restaurant, changed its name to Lobstah's and have revamped the menu. I am told that the Maine lobsters, fresh out of their own tank, feature in the Lazy Garlic Lobster Casserole, the Lobster Pot Pie and the Lobster Boil for Two are outstanding. As an alterna-tive you might like to try their Maryland Style Crab Cakes which, if you are a crab cake person like me, are to die for. Wash these choices down with a southern style Mint Julep and your gastronomical adventure is complete. Both of these establishments have other terrific sea food dishes that will make your taste buds salivate just by reading the menu. So shake a tail feather and join them for dinner. It is said that eighty percent of new restaurants fail within their first year of business. However, a large percentage of this is usually when it is the owner's first business venture. In the case of the two previously mentioned restaurants, these owners are seasoned professionals and have had ample business experience. Both are well aware of the pitfalls, that can be encountered in this business, and this should keep them on a rock solid business footing.

Another local businessman, with great vision, is Bill Herlihy the proprietor of the Bridge Street Bistro. His upstairs restaurant was quite successful but Bill felt that too many people were not aware of its location. In a stroke of shear brilliance he decided to utilize the ground level parking area and set up a large bar with entertainment, right on the corner of Bridge Street and Gulf of Mexico Drive. He brought in some of the best entertainers in Manatee County and there is no way that anyone can miss it now. On weekends it is standing room only as the crowds pack in to enjoy the exciting atmosphere. He has named this new venture Island Time Bar and Grill and dining is also available here now. Their grassy key grouper, veal picatta and mahi mahi fish entrée are exceptional. On the lighter side their maple salmon teriyaki salad will complete an exceptional dining experience. All the entertainment is first class but my particular favorite is the Ted Stevens and the Doo Shots. Ted plays a great guitar and is ably backed by a driving drummer and a pulsating stand up base. This Rock-a-Billy trio, much in the style of the Brian Setzer Stray Cats, has the crowd jumping and jiving the night away.

Just over the bridge and back on the main land, at Cortez village, a Trading Post has just opened up. This interests me greatly because up until now the only ways to get rid of unwanted household items, has been to donate them to a Goodwill store or to hold your own yard sale. If you donate them you are basically giving them away free and some items, although no longer needed, still have some value. Holding a yard sale is a lot of work because not only does it take time to price all the items, set them all out and then you have to work on it for the best part of two days. The last time I did a yard sale at the end, because of the steamy conditions, I was completely worn out. The trading post is basically a shop where a person can just go in and buy any item as in a regular store. They have furniture, carpets, art works, jewelry, clothing and a multitude of good quality merchandise. However, what I like is that they also offer a bartering system whereby you can take in an item and they will take it off your hands and give you barter dollars in return. I no longer use a coal fire and so I took in a fire grate set of tools, which had been standing in my tool shed for around four or five years. In all fairness if they think that they can sell your item, for a particular price, they will give you half of that in barter dollars. This beats, by a long shot, what I would get for the same item at a yard sale where people want to pay you as little as humanly possible. With the money from the tool set I bought myself a very nice silver ring with an eagle embossed on it.

Because I will soon be leaving on a trip to Ireland, and it will certainly be colder and possibly wetter, I also bought a long retro-styled black soft textured leather coat. This I obtained by taking in several other items that have been idly hanging around in my tool shed for a considerable period of time. I really like the barter system and I have frequently used it myself when selling our books. I usually carry copies of our books with me when we are in a bar, restaurant or café setting, incase people are interested in buying them. I quite frequently will trade our books to someone who will, in turn, pick up our bar tab. This is no different from them giving me the money for the books and me then taking that same money to pay my bill. It just seems to make perfect sense to me and when I have offered, this payment alternative method, I have rarely ever been turned down. Particularly in such a situation where the conviviality is flowing like wine. It has been said, by those in the know, that only rock stars and sports idols have more fun than I and with my mantra of"Sax, Rugs and Sausage Rolls,"who can doubt it.

I do not want to labor the point but, as I have said before, there is a good deal of people on this island that have money to spare. Because of this there is another strange phenomenon that quite often occurs here and that is the practice of replacing furniture and placing the older items at the road side curb for anyone to claim. Many of the houses, apartments and condominiums here are sold as a"turn key"deal. That means that they are fully furnished, from top to bottom, mainly because the seller does not want the added aggravation of having to sell off all these items themselves in a piece meal fashion. The seller just adds the cost of all the furniture to the price for the accommodation. The buyers, on the other hand, are more interested in the property location than the furnishings and so they buy the property "as is"for the time being.

Now there comes a time, down the road a little, when the new owners are settled into their new corner of paradise and decide to refurbish the accommodation. At this stage they just put all the unwanted items out by the side of the curb for any passer-by to take on a first come first served basis. If I had owned a truck I swear that I could have refurnished my whole house on these rare unannounced occasions. I openly admit that I have been the recipient of a nice number of smaller items but it is difficult to get a three piece bedroom set into a Volks Wagon Beetle. If an alert person, on this island, had some storage space at home he could collect these items, put an advertisement in the local newspaper and make a tidy profit from reselling them. After all most of these items are classed as"gently used"and would be perfectly acceptable to their new owners. Who said that the age of the entrepreneur was dead?

I knew of a man once, back in England, who had a large hole in the ground on his rural property. He did a deal with his local government whereby they could use his hole as a land fill. Several years later he did a deal, with the same people, to buy back the waste that they had put in his hole in the ground. Apparently, they now wanted to build a new road and needed that landfill refuse as a foundation on which the cement would now be poured. This guy got them coming and going and this is just about the best incident of"having your cake and eating it too"that I have ever heard. So chalk one up for the little guy as it appears that there is justice in the world after all.

Added to the above redistribution of house furnishings, visitors also leave a good amount of beach items such as tents, chairs, inflatable floating devises and various other temporary amusement items which are discarded as the owners have no way to get them home. They cannot take them on a plane and their cars are usually filled to the gunnels and, having served their purpose, they are deliberately disguarded. Then there are the items which are unintentionally lost, such as sun glasses, reading glasses, beach towels, balls, buckets and spades, which all makes beach combing a profitable pass time on this island. These activities quite often resemble an Arabian market place.

Graeme Edge, one of the founding members of the British rock band The Moody Blues, also has a business interest on this island. Although he lives in Bradenton, just off the island, he owns a motel/guest house here in Bradenton Beach named the Linger Longer. When I first came down here to live, around thirteen years ago, Sharon and I were in the habit of walking the beach at sundown. One evening we would go up the island and the next night we would walk down the beach. Going south, just past the Moose Lodge, was a row of small houses. A year or two after we arrived here we noticed that some guy had bought two of them and had then set about converting them into one larger rental accommodation, We would quite often see the owner doing his rounds, at the end of the day, to see what progress had been made. Little did we know that this person was the famous Graeme Edge. I wondered why he was always singing Nights in White Satin. Of course, like me, he has a crop of gray hair and has filled out a little from his former and more illustrious days. Never the less, his voice is still good enough for him to perform on the occasional Moody Blues reunion tour. I am also told that, from time to time, he can be persuaded to perform with some of our local musicians whenever a worthy benefit jam session is arranged. We have an abundance of good musicians in this area some of whom are local born and others who, for some reason or another, have gravitated to this extraordinary, free-spirited location.

Nineteen

Cyber Fiber

Computers have become an integral part of our daily lives and they have brought, to us all, many modern day advantages which have enhanced our lives a great deal. Unfortunately it did not take long for the dishonest people, of the world, to devise intricate schemes that allows them to enter our lives uninvited. They have set about trying, and in many cases succeeding, to rob us of what is rightly ours. In days gone by these criminals had to sneak up on us and physically attack us but not any longer. They can now recline in the comfort or their own dwellings and, without breaking a sweat, they can press computer keys and enter our lives without our knowledge. Without exerting themselves these callous creeps can wangle their way into people's lives with the sole intension of robbing them with one phony ruse or another. They don't even need to look you in the face, nor even have to be in the same country, all they have to do is jiggle some computer keys and, with any amount of good fortune on their part, they can steal an honest person's life savings in the blink of an eye.

The other day our bedside phone rang and because it was not even 9:00 AM yet I did not pick up. Usually at that hour of the morning only telemarketers call and so I just listened to the message. It was from a business associate of Sharon's who had just received her e-mail. Supposedly she was stranded, in London, England, and was asking for him to send $1800, to a post box there, so that she could pay her hotel bill and buy a flight ticket back to the USA. The e-mail went on to say that she had been robbed of all her money and credit cards and was begging for help.

Since Sharon was right there with me, at our home in Bradenton Beach, Florida and would never travel outside of America without me, this was an obvious hoax. The most distressing thing about this was that this imposter had hacked into our e-mail account and sent this same bogus plea to everyone who was on our e-mail list. Luckily the guy who tipped us off, to this scam, had seen this type of fraud before and knew immediately that it smelled fishy. However, with bitter consternation, for the next three days we were inundated with phone calls, from friends from all over the world, asking if this was true or not and thank goodness no-one was taken in by this dishonest ploy. However, a lady friend of Sharon's, who lives up near Cleveland, Ohio, was almost taken in but when she asked her son to help her send the money, he recognized the ruse for what it was. The other galling fact is that, because of all this dishonesty, we have had to change our e-mail address and our security pass word, which is a total inconvenience as it now means having to print new business cards. I watched a television documentary once that showed people, who happened to be in Nigeria, Africa, spending virtually every hour of every day doing nothing else but trying to hack into other peoples accounts from around the world. Apparently, if they can get their hands on any disused or discarded computer, they have the know how to retrieve all the information contained there in. All discarded computers, there fore, should be crushed as is the practice with scrapped automobiles.

The above incident is the fourth time, in a period of two months, that we have been the victim of a possible on-line scam. We have received a plea from someone in Africa, where apparently a good deal of scams are originated, saying that they have a large amount of money there and for the lack of a down payment fee, they cannot access their fortune. They then ask for you to wire them the money for which they will split their fortune with you. Some of these ruses are so blatantly flawed that ninety nine percent of people will immediately see through them. However, it only takes two or three gullible people, who are usually elderly, for the perpetrator to be sitting pretty. On another occasion I was informed, by e-mail, that I had won some lottery in England, which I had not even entered. The options which this bogus company gave me was to send them a fee to cover the expense, of getting the winnings to me. If I would send an amount of $1500 they would send me the winnings. The other option was to fly over and collect the winnings from them in person and when I opted to do this, the communications ceased and I never heard from them again.

Sharon was also informed that she could be employed, by some company or other, as a secret shopper and all she had to do is cash a cheque that they would send her and send half of that amount back to them by Federal Express. She received the cheque which we took to our bank where, as we suspected, it was pronounced as bogus. We then took the cheque and turned it over to the Post Office for them to investigate. Would you believe that this guy, who sounded as if he was from India, had the gall to phone us and say that we had stolen his cheque and that he was going to inform the FBI. When I told him not to bother because the FBI were already looking for him, there was a sudden"click"on the end of the line Once again we never heard from that person again but his impertinent attitude just goes to show how brazen these people are and how they can brow beat a lesser informed dupe to accept some of these dirty deals.

Incidentally, the cheque that this particular guy sent Sharon looked, in every sense of the word, to be real and authentic in almost every detail. So never try and cash one of these cleverly disguised pieces of counterfeit without having a bank official verify it first as it is better to be safe than sorry. Since we have been singled out so often, in such a short space of time. I wonder whether or not these computer crooks network with each other and swap lists of people that they can possibly dupe. Once they have got you in their sights they will not give up trying to put your money into their bank accounts. Therefore, beware of strangers bearing false gifts and be alert so that, if you become a target of fraud, your security system and your common sense is not compromised. If it seems too good to be true, it more than likely is and never believe that you have won money from some enterprise that you have not contributed to. No-one gives money away juat for the heck of it.

Twenty
Nature's Wrath

Tropical storm Debby passed by us last week on her way up to the Florida Pan Handle and, oh boy, did she make herself known here on our island. She left a trail of devastation, that affected so many people, here on the western shores of Florida. Debby headed due north right up the Gulf of Mexico about two hundred miles west of our location. Unfortunately she stalled for three days, northwest of us, exactly where it would produce the worst possible conditions on Anna Maria Island. Because of where the eye of the storm was located and because it was revolving in an anti clockwise direction this meant that we were right on its south east outer edge. As the storm rotated northwards it brought sixty mile an hour winds off the ocean and torrential rains which flooded many parts of the island. Normally this type of weather passes through in about twenty four hours but with it being stalled for three days we had more rain than we could normally handle.

Added to all this the rains came at the exact time of the month as did the Gulf's high tides and so we were being flooded from both the sea and the skies. This devastation affected the western coast of Florida from Port Charlotte in the south to Cedar Key in the north with many homes and vehicles being flooded and their occupants having to be evacuated by boat. We, on the other hand, were quite lucky with only my outside yard being flooded with a small manageable amount of rain penetrating my shingled roof. I was able to catch the driving rain in small containers and I have since gone up onto the roof and sealed those areas which I felt were weak. Some of my garden plants perished as they were not salt tolerant and the high winds also brought down quite a few branches from my palms and various other trees. It took the better part of a week to put my yard back to somewhere near its former glory.

Where Debby was at her most destructive was on the beaches of our coast line. The thunderous waves took huge bites out of the shore line and when it was all over the beaches had been robbed of at least three foot of sand. However, the sand loss in the south half of the island turned out to be a bonus for the beaches on the north end. Since the prevailing storm was coming from the southwest, the enormous waves wash the sand north-wards and our loss became their gain. The south beaches are now left with jagged protruding rocks, which had been hidden below the sand for many years but were now fully exposed all along the beaches. The only small blessings are that it is now easier to find fossilized shark's teeth which hopefully will be thrown up from their long time resting places. I am also now able to retrieve some of the smaller jagged rocks and use them to decorate my front yard. This proves the theory that even a blind pig gets an acorn once in a while.

Even more devastating though was the affect that the storm had on the local wild life. Literally hundreds of shore bird and turtle nests, estimated at eighty percent of this years crop, were destroyed with almost a whole years supply of eggs and hatch-lings being washed away. What a pity because it had just been reported that a record number of nests had been recently counted and this would have boosted our wild life population for years to come. Several local people had their boats sunk and for some of them this was a crushing blow because their boats were also their homes. All of the beach side restaurants and cafes had to build make shift steps or stairs so that people could access the property by ascending them from the beaches. About six years ago Manatee County spent ten million dollars to refurbish the beaches, out here on these barrier islands. In three days Mother Nature has returned the beaches to their natural positions. When I lived in Britain the weather was temperate and it wasn't until I came to America that I have experienced the raw energy of nature at its most foreboding.

During the summer months, here in Florida, we have spasmodic heavy rain showers which can leave several inches of water standing on the ground. The rain also fills up any upturned yard vessels and these can become a breeding ground for, that pest of all pests, the mosquito. They lay their lava in any standing water and if not closely controlled, with their habit of biting people, this could produce an acute problem. The Florida Department of Natural Resources, however, has come up with a unique system for dealing with these pesky varmints. They breed dragon flies, in captivity, and during night time they drop thousands of these useful creatures from helicopters and, with their avarice for eating mosquitoes, the problem is taken care of by natural methods. Most people hardly even notice this procedure with the possible exception of visitors who, from time to time, might comment on the fact that they have observed an unusual number of dragon flies. In this case man has intervened, to assist nature, in solving one of its own intrinsic problems and this is to be lauded. Such ingenuity is the spice of life and we must now endeavor to use similar technologies to eat up oil spills so that our oceans can stay pollutant free. Every available assistance should be given to eliminate this blight because to be able to solve this problem would be a blessing indeed.

At this very moment, while we are experiencing all these storms, the state of Colorado is experiencing the worst wild fires in that State's history. In the region of Colorado Springs in, would you believe, Hope County there has been twenty seven square miles of land completely devastated around Waldo Canyon. In Colorado, to keep its naturally pristine appearance, houses are built within and around the many pine trees that thrive at those altitudes. For most of the time this is beautiful with man and nature existing in harmony. However, there is one exception and that is during forest fires. The flames literally leap from tinder dry tree to tree at such a pace that it fuels the wild fire and eats up acres of land in mere minutes. Any tree lined houses, in the vicinity of this horrific incident, are also eaten up by the intense heat and are literally burned to the ground. Whole towns and subdivisions are being wiped off the map with families losing everything that they once owned. Flooding can sometimes be devastating but eventually, after some hardships, the water subsides and people can get back to normal because their houses are still standing. After Debby had her wicked way with our lives just two days of sunshine sapped up all the rain soaked grounds and we were almost back to normal.

With wild fires, being whipped up by strong winds, family homes and their entire contents can be incinerated with the owner's total belongings destroyed and life style being changed forever. After this type of disaster the recovery road is long and arduous and in some cases people never completely recover. This must be such a crushing body blow and how anyone can recover from such an horrendous freak of nature is beyond my wildest imagination. To date these persistent fires have been running amok for almost three weeks and unfortunately it has been reported that twenty seven people have died so far and many more still unaccounted for. America is such a great and vast country that it can sometimes experience the best of times and the worst of times all in the same moment. Living here is not for the faint of heart and if people are of the type that need everything to be in apple pie order then they should think long and hard before making the decision to live in these rugged yet still barely civilized regions. Perhaps a more cultured setting such as one of America's huge metropolises, where the deer and the antelope do not roam, would be more to their liking. It is just a little over one hundred odd years ago that settlers were still fighting off wild Indians and animals to survive on a daily basis. A person still has to be as tough as nails to survive in some of the outlying areas of the USA.. The deserts, the mountains and the swamps all come with their own brand of natural survivalists and these critters are not always well disposed of having to share their domain with human interlopers. It is much better to be fore warned and thus fore armed about the perils that go with living off the beaten track.

As a "for instance" there was an incident that happened around a month ago in Everglade City about one hundred miles south of my home. Apparently one of the airboat captains was showing off to his passengers by feeding an alligator by hand, which incidentally is illegal. He would raise his arm outside of the airboat and dangle a piece of chicken so that the alligator would come up out of the water and snatch it. The usual method of feeding alligators is to throw the meat into the water but this captain, probably in an attempt to get more tips, decided otherwise. With all the passengers watching the alligator, in a split second, arose out of the water and bit the captains hand clean off. You can imagine the frantic scene that ensued as the passengers launched into panic mode in an attempt to take the captain to get emergency medical attention. Alligator hunters were called in and as always, in a case like this, they captured the offending alligator, killed it, cut its stomach open and retrieved the hand. They then packed the dismembered hand in a cooler full of ice and took it immediately to join the rest of the captain, at a nearby hospital, in the hope that it could be reattached. Up in the Rockies a hiker was badly mauled by a grizzly bear when he inadvertently walked between the she bear and her cub. Even though badly wounded the hiker managed to climb a tree where he stayed, for forty eight hours, until he was found there by a search party. He narrowly escaped with his life and I am guessing that it will be a long time, if ever, that he will hike alone up in the mountains. I do not relate these stories to scare people stiff but just to illuminate them to a fact that a beautiful day can turn into hell if a person drops his guard for even one minute. Nature can, on times, have reckless disregard for the well being of mankind and safety of the human race.

Most non-Americans associate this country with Disney World, Las Vegas or perhaps the big tourist cities like New York, Washington, Los Angeles or Miami. However, if they become more adventurous and go to places like the Grand Canyon, the Painted Desert, the Florida Everglades or even any of the many National Parks they must know, even before they plan to visit, that these places have hardly changed from hundreds of years ago and must be taken seriously. As the motto of the Boy Scouts proclaims"be prepared"at all times. In remote places, such as these, a good dog with its acute sense of smell is essential because it will alert a person to impending danger long before it happens. So, now that you have been forewarned, come on over and enjoy the vast and rugged beauty of America. It is still a most entrancing place to be and, if you keep an open mind, you will be amazed as to the shear wonderment of it all. The incidents which I have related are rare but, never the less, no-one would want to find themselves in one of these unenviable circumstances. I am sure that millions of visitors come to America without incidents such as these and have a simply wonderful time and long may that tradition continue.

Twenty One
Island to Ireland

I have just returned from my much heralded trip to Ireland which, in spite of the mid summer cost, turned out to be a wonderful experience. My last visit to the Erin Isle was way back in 1976 but this was to be Sharon's very first occasion of setting foot on this still fascinating place known affectionately as "The Old Sod". Our main objective was to attend the wedding of Matt Metcalfe to Edel Brady in the County Tyrone town of Sion Mills. We decided to fly from the States directly into the capitol of Dublin and then catch a bus from there to Londonderry which was a four hour trip through County Monaghan, Tyrone and then County Derry. This afforded us the chance to see parts that we would not normally come anywhere near to. From the center of Londonderry it was but a three minute taxi ride to our temporary home, called the Iona Inn which, just so happened to be, located on the Water Side of town. This put us within two miles of the Everglades Hotel where the wedding reception was to be held. It seemed superfluous to me that someone from Florida should stay at a hotel with a Floridian name. Besides at the Iona Inn instead of staying at a hotel with a bar we had a room directly over a bar, which seemed to make perfect sense to me.

Lyn Clarke

The bar beneath the Iona was called Moran's and the owners Tom and Molly's family have owned this business since 1960.. When I visited The Everglades Hotel it became clear to me that most, if not all, of the patrons were from out of town whereas at the Iona the patrons were all, with the exception of us, local people. So in no time at all they clued me in on all the local news and details of the surrounding area. Sharon and I walked across the main bridge to Londonderry's city center with its impressive protective city walls. Also the poignant statue of two boys from opposite sides of the River Foyle, shaking hands in an act of unity, was an encouraging sign of how far this city has progressed. In the very center of the city there was a huge flat screen set up outdoors with chairs available so that passers by could relax, in the sunshine, and take in the Olympic Games from London. What with sandwiches and coffee available it was just like sitting in your own living room with a bunch of friendly strangers. The Irish folk and the entertainment was first class and they were more than hospitable and ready to make us feel at home. I have to say that I have visited many cities in Europe but Londonderry is a most pleasant place to be on a beautiful summer's day.

On the Sunday, following the wedding, we visited the city again, this time with my son, daughter and grandson, who had arrived at Larne via the car ferry from Stranraer in Scotland. After a second walk around the city, which included a Blue Grass festival where we were entertained by a very good up and coming Irish band called The Farriers, we decided to bring the car over from Water Side. This time we walked across the newer pedestrian Peace Bridge with its ess-shaped construction. My family had come over to join us and that night we all went for a departure meal, with all the out of town wedding guests, which included a whole slew of Matt's friends from the Wirral area of Cheshire.

On Saturday, the day of the wedding, we all congregated at the Everglades hotel where a fleet of cars whisked us down to the church at Sion Mills. The wedding itself was just about as perfect as any girl could possibly dream of having. Catholic weddings do tend to run longer than most others, that I have attended, yet nothing detracted from the sheer bliss of the occasion. The bride was, of course, beautiful and radiant and the groom was altogether bold and handsome making the perfect couple. With the ceremony completed it was photograph time and then back into the fleet of cars and on to the reception back at the Everglades.

The excited guests were greeted with complimentary drinks while awaiting the entrance of the happy couple. From there it was into the main hall for a sumptuous sit down three course meal. After a short recess where the guests had time to relax and in my case, have a quick nap, the live music band was ready to get the event well and truly started and at which point mayhem let loose. To get everyone in the right mood the band began with"Galway Girl"which, as it just so happened, is currently one of my favorite Irish tunes. Everybody jumped up and onto the dance floor for a night of riotous and flagrant dancing. I must confess that towards the end of the evening I was not at my riotous best because of my previous night's activities, 'till three-o-clock in the morning at Moran's Bar, took its toll.

One small unsavory incident occurred when the act of someone pestering me, by alternatively tapping on each of my shoulders from behind, resulted in me swinging my fist backwards over my head. I hit the unknown joker right square in the mouth and, to my utter dismay, it turned out to be the grooms eighty six year old grandfather. Luckily for me, I had known him for many years and it was all taken as a typical Taffy cock-up. Anyone who has known me, for any length of time, should expect such retribution as my tolerance for being messed with is historically short. My apologies go out to any and all offended parties but, thus face it, no wedding party is complete unless at least one unrehearsed diabolical incident takes place. What I frequently have to ask myself is"Why does this type of incident always happen to be me ?"

On the Sunday evening, after the farewell party, my daughter Louise drove all of our family the sixty odd miles to Bush Mills, up on the rugged coast of County Antrim. Here she had rented us a comfortably house where Louise, Richard, Jack, Sharon and I spent the next six days exploring Antrim beautiful shore line. The weather was uncommonly warm and sunny and we ere told, by the locals, that it was the best weather of the whole year to date. Because of this we were able to visit Castle Rock, Port Stewart, Port Rush, White Rocks, Ballycastle and The distillery at Bush Mills. I went to Royal Port Rush Golf Club, the home of the most recent Irish Open Tournament and bought a good Michigan friend of mine two club head covers. To say that this place was expensive is an under statement and to give an example they were selling sweaters for two hundred and forty five British pounds, or around four hundred U S dollars. However, in all fairness, they did give me a handful of free monogrammed tees to soften the shock. We would liked to have gone by boat to Rathlin Island but we were told that the puffins, Sharon's favorite birds, had already flown from the isle making this trip less than appealing.

Apart from all this we also visited the ruins of Dunluce Castle and found it to be as good as any other that I have seen throughout Wales, Scotland or England. We visited the rope bridge at Carrick-a-Rede which spans over to a rock with an eighty five foot drop into the Atlantic Ocean. I must confess that although I was there I did not cross the bridge as my stomach was in turmoil and any unaccounted delays could have proved fatal for all concerned. However I have saved the best for last and this was our visit to the Giant's Causeway. If there is such a thing as a list of the seven most natural mind bending things to see, this has to be on it. Formed during a volcanic eruption, when the continents divided three hundred thousand years ago, these strange hexagonal basalt columns are unique. The columns are so perfectly intertwined that it appears like a perfectly laid roman road which, one can only assume, is man made. The only thing wrong with that assumption is that the hexagonal pieces are so large that it would take a giant to make it happen. The columns are higher at the mountain side and taper downwards to the ocean and continues out under the sea which gives it the appearance of a natural causeway, hence its obvious name. This sight is on a par with Ayers Rock in Australia or Machu Picchu in Peru and simply has to be seen to be believed.

Exactly one week, from the day of the wedding, it was farewell to Ulster as we left Bush Mills. Sharon and I took a taxi to Coleraine to catch a bus to Belfast and from there another bus on to Dublin while Louise, Richard and Jack drove back to Larne to take the ferry back over to the main land. Unbeknown to us, on arriving at Colerain, there as a large band assembling with drums, flutes, accordions and flags waving in the breeze. They all passed us as we drove into town and as we alighted the bus they passed us again. They marched with great pomp and purpose as if their lives depended on it and I stood there completely mystified. I asked a little old lady as to where they were going and she answered that they were off to Londonderry. Knowing, in my mind, that Londonderry was some sixty miles away I asked with some trepidation"They are marching all the way to Londonderry?"To which she replied, with a twinkle in her eye"No, they are going around the corner to get on a bus". Apparently it was the anniversary of when the siege of Londonderry was broken, some two hundred and fifty years ago and, to this very day, it is still celebrated. With my upbringing I am a"Proddy-dog"but if people, with opposite views to mine, came marching through my neighborhood in this manner, I would be incensed to the verge of anger. Every other town that we passed through that day had a similar marching band going off to Londonderry for the same celebration. Let us hope that the memories of Bloody Sunday are buried for good.

From Coleraine our bus went through Ballymoney, Ballymena, passing by the beautiful town of Portglenone, and then on to Antrim before arriving at Belfast. Just enough time there for a cup of coffee and a pork pie and we were away by bus to Dublin. We were dropped off at the main airport and with a quick taxi ride we were at our hotel at Swords a suburb about fifteen miles from downtown Dublin. For the next two days we were without a car and so we stayed right there with the shopping area only a fifteen minute walk away. We found a good pub, Smyth's Cock Tavern [excuse my language] where we encamped while eating, supping and finding out, from the locals, what was going on.

The next afternoon, the day before we had to depart, we were at the Forty Four Main Street Bar to hear some good old traditional Irish music and we were not let down. People randomly sat in with guitars, banjos, hand drums and accordions, or just sang, as the whole joint shook with excitement. When this impromptu session finished,around nine in the evening, we moved a few doors down the street to a place which I think, when told to me with a severe accent, was called the Slaughter House. Here we enjoyed some modern rock and roll provided by a group of exceptional musicians known as The Darogh Bouggies. Two of them Pat"Ditch"Cassidy, minus the Sundance Kid, had sung with the famous band Tin Lizzie and his gravelly voice was riveting. Guitar player Greg McClathie had played with The Shadows and had also backed Dusty Springfield. and his solo in the middle of Pink Floyd's"Brick in the Wall"was as near to perfect as I have ever heard. The base guitar player Jay Malone could come to America tomorrow and make money right away. The whole evening took a pivotal turn when a young lady soprano, named Ciara Moran, stood up and sang the operatic aria"Pia Jesus"She turned the previous baying crowd into a transfixed silence and then finished to an explosion of applause normally provided exclusively for divas. Sharon and I sat on a sofa, a mere three feet from the artists, without having to pay one single penny.

On our last day in Eire, Sharon and I were walking back from Swords to our hotel when I noticed a clump of shamrocks growing on the grass verge near the roadside. This was a most unlikely place, right in front of a residential house, to see this wild plant but never-the-less there they were. As I kept walking Sharon stopped just as I was telling her that to find a four leaved shamrock was very rare and considered extremely lucky. I also told her not to waste her time as many had tried and many had failed. I am not kidding you when I say that, within no more than two minutes, she stood up and said "You mean like this?" Would you believe it, she was standing there holding up a four leaved shamrock. This somewhat proves the theory that if you believe enough that something is possible, then it very likely is. Sharon throughout her life in America had, at different times, searched for a four leaved clover but never was successful. Here in the Emerald Isle, where it seems all things are possible, she had finally achieved her goal. There is no other way to say it other than"That's Ireland for you. ' I am beginning to think that just maybe Leprechauns really do exist.

A great example of typical Irish humor.

Lyn and Sharon at Irish wedding.

Clarke...Lyn Clarke.

Lyn at Giants Causeway.

Lyn at Bush Mills, County Atrium.

Our hostess, Mollie at Iona Inn, Londonderry.

Read All of Lyn Clarke's Chronicles
All titles currently in print. Coming soon to eBook

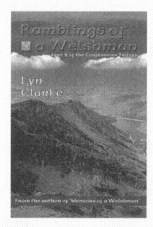

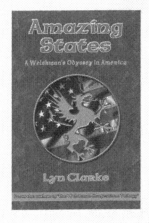

Also in eBook

Made in the USA
Columbia, SC
27 November 2018